The Coronavirus Pandemic

An English Perspective

by Dr David Holding

First published by
Words are Life, 2022
www.wordsarelife.co.uk

First published in Great Britain in 2022 by
Words are Life
10 Chester Place,
Adlington, Chorley, PR6 9RP
wordsarelife@mail.com
www.wordsarelife.co.uk

Electronic version and paperback versions available for
purchase on Amazon.

Acknowledgements

In writing a work of this nature, the researcher is faced with several obstacles since the subject of the work was previously an 'unknown quantity'. Its appearance on the global stage was unexpected and certainly unprecedented. Consequently, few published works or accounts relating to this particular pandemic exist. However, from a positive view, this enables the researcher to pursue a wealth of current contemporaneous material in the form of government papers and media articles, including a wealth of statistical data about COVID-19 since its appearance in England in 2020 – and up to the present time.

It has been virtually impossible to express personal thanks to the many individuals who have assisted my research. There have been people who have provided me with 'first hand' accounts of the impact of COVID on their own working lives. These have included NHS staff at all levels of the service, together with GP practices. I also acknowledge the input from academic colleagues representing various disciplines and am grateful for the provision of data from the numerous organisations I have consulted, including local authorities, media contacts and a few politicians. To all these generous people, my gratitude losses no sincerity in its generality.

Lastly, but never least, the one individual I can thank individually, and indeed take great pleasure in so doing, is my ever-supportive publisher, Lesley Atherton. Lesley is and continues to be the firm foundation upon which I have safely built my works over several years. Long may that foundation endure.

Dr David Holding, 2021

About the Author

Dr David Holding studied history at Manchester University before entering the teaching profession in the 1970s. He taught in both state and independent sectors. During this time, he continued historical research culminating in both a Master's degree and a Doctorate. Having previously studied law, David gained a Master of Law degree in Medical Law, which enabled him to transfer to teaching legal courses at university. Since retiring, David has concentrated his research and writing on various aspects of local history, legal trials, forensic science and medico-legal topics.

Also by David Holding

Murder in the Heather: The Winter Hill Murder of 1838
This book is a unique account of a brutal murder that occurred on the summit of Winter Hill in Lancashire in 1838. The account draws on both contemporary media reports and court transcripts and examines the events leading to the killing of a 21-year-old packman. It details the trial proceedings of the only suspect in the case. The work concludes with a re-assessment of the case in the light of modern forensic investigation. The reader is invited to reach their own 'verdict' based on the evidence provided.

The Pendle Witch Trials of 1612
The book provides readers with a sequential overview of the famous chain of events that ultimately led to the execution of women accused of practising witchcraft in the county of Lancashire. It is presented as a chronological account of the famous trials at Lancaster Castle in 1612. This book introduces the evidence and interview transcripts that formed the major plank of the prosecution case and will appeal to both the general reader and local historian.

The Dark Figure: Crime in Victorian Bolton
This book provides an absorbing overview of crime in the Lancashire town of Bolton over the period 1850 to 1890. It is primarily based on documentary survey and analysis of court and police records covering the period. It assesses changes in crime over time and asks whether these relate to economic, social or political changes taking place at the same time. The reader is left to reflect on whether crime (in all its many forms) has changed over time.

Bleak Christmas: The Pretoria Colliery Disaster of 1910
This work charts the events of the Lancashire Pretoria Pit disaster in December 1910. It reflects on the devastation it left to many local communities whose main source of employment was coal. The main sources analysed are the Home Office Report on the disaster and the Report of the Inquest. The findings of these detailed legal reports are presented in a format that will supplement existing material on the event. The book will also provide a reference source for both local historians and the interested general reader.

Doctors in the Dock: The Trials of Doctors Harold Shipman, John Bodkin Adams and Buck Ruxton
This book takes the reader on a journey into the world of three medical doctors in England, each coming from a different social background but with one common thread going through their lives. They all stood trial for murder. In each case, the reader is presented with all relevant evidence available to jurors in the case. The overall aim of this work is to invite readers to exercise their judgment in reaching a verdict.

Forensic Science Basics: Every Contact Leaves a Trace
This work is an absorbing introductory study of the techniques familiar from numerous trials, media reports and TV crime dramas. It begins with the basic principles of forensic science then examines such aspects as the time of death, causes of death, weapons of crime, identification of offenders and much more. It provides essential reading for those who wish to gain a basic introduction to this fascinating area of science.

A Warning from History: The Influenza Pandemic of 1918
The 1918 Influenza Pandemic was one of the most deadly events in human history, and understanding the events and experience of 1918 is of great importance to pandemic preparation. This book aims to address questions concerning the pandemic's origin, features and causes to provide the reader with an appreciation of the 1918 pandemic and its implications for future pandemics. This work caters to both the science-orientated and general reader in this crucial area of global and public health.

The Lady Chatterley Trial Revisited
The 1960 obscenity trial of Lady Chatterley's Lover remains a symbol of freedom of expression. It is also a seminal case in British literary and social history and credited as the catalyst which encouraged frank discussion of sexual behaviour. This book introduces readers to the trial itself, describing the prosecution and defence opening and closing speeches to the jury, and much more before culminating in the judge's summing-up and the final verdict. The reader is provided with all the evidence to reach a considered assessment of the case and a question to consider – can certain literature 'actually' corrupt, or does it simply encourage expensive court trials and boost sales?

The Oscar Wilde Trials Revisited
It is only given to very few people to be the principal figure in three Old Bailey trials, before three different judges, and at three consecutive

court sessions, all in one year. This complexity is one of the fascina-
tions of the 1895 Oscar Wilde trials. In addition, they embodied
celebrity, sex, humorous dialogue, outstanding displays of advocacy,
political intrigue woven with issues of art and morality. Wilde's prosecution of the Marquess of Queensberry from criminal libel, and Wilde's
later prosecution for 'gross indecency', reveal a complex person at odds
with a class-centred and morally ambiguous Victorian society. This
work considers these famous trials in chronological sequence and in-
vites the reader to participate as an observer and potential juror in the
proceedings. Finally, the reader is encouraged to consider the evidence
presented at each trial and arrive at their own conclusions. This work
will be of particular interest to law students owing to the counsel's skil-
fully demonstrated advocacy skills. It also caters for the general reader
with a particular interest in the presentation of criminal cases in the
courts in England.

The Whitechapel Murders of 1888
The killing of five women in the Whitechapel area of East London in
1888 remains the greatest and most horrendous of all unsolved murder
mysteries. It is the classic 'Cold Case'. This work takes a novel look
into the case from the perspective of the criminal investigation itself. In
this approach, the more speculative and conspiracy theories surrounding the 'Jack the Ripper' crimes have been avoided. The reader is
offered insights into these murders by employing the modern forensic
techniques of geographical and offender profiling, which shed new
light on these serial killings.

Forensic Pathology Basics: The Dead Do Tell a Story
In this work, the reader is taken on a sequential journey of discovery
into the fascinating world of Forensic Pathology, with no previous
knowledge of the subject being required of readers. Beginning with the
initial discovery of a body, the reader experiences the processes involving the forensic pathologist, from the initial examination and identification of the deceased to the final autopsy. The reader will be introduced to practical applications of the pathologist's skills and techniques
at each stage. Past criminal cases will be introduced to demonstrate the
variety of scenarios in which the assistance of the forensic pathologist
is vital. The overall aim of this work is to provide the reader with a fascinating insight into the largely unseen involvement of the forensic
pathologist in death investigations. It is especially fascinating when the
circumstances involve criminal activity. The manner and causes of
death are discussed in detail and cover the main areas of injury. A

glossary of medical terminology is provided to explain the various terms used in the text. The work concludes with a Selected Bibliography to enable the reader to pursue their research in those areas they find particularly interesting and relevant.

Contents

Introduction

This work aims to provide the reader with an easily accessible yet comprehensive account of the unprecedented and unexpected emergence of the coronavirus in England from 2020 to the present time.

This pandemic arrived in England in early January 2020 and brought in its wake a devastating impact upon the social and economic life of the country. The world was ill-prepared for such a pandemic, with the threat it posed to health on an unimaginable global scale. While this work is primarily focused upon England's response to the threat, this does not diminish the effects of this pandemic upon the other three countries that constitute the United Kingdom.

Scotland, Wales and Northern Ireland have their own devolved governments and constitutions. Consequently, their approach and policies for dealing with the threat have differed only in applying those policies, never in their intent to suppress COVID-19's spread. As in England, these governments experienced the tragic loss of life and upheaval to their respective social and economic structures. There has been (and I believe still is) a 'united' effort and response to suppress the progress of COVID-19 throughout the United Kingdom.

This work is organised into five chapters, each examining a specific aspect of the pandemic in England. Chapter One provides the reader with the background and epidemiology of the coronavirus and its emerging variants. It also examines the theories regarding the 'origins' of COVID-19, some of which are still controversial.

The second chapter analyses the impact on three prime areas of English society: Health and Social Care, Education and the Economy. It questions the government's strategies to control the virus at the expense of these other essential social services.

The third chapter examines the race to produce vaccines to combat the rising tide of COVID. It also pays tribute to the vaccine programme's success in vastly reducing the incidence of infection throughout the country.

Chapter Four is devoted to analysing the vast amount of statistical data generated in response to the pandemic and the requirement to monitor its progress daily. It also explains the relevance of the 'R' number in informing government policy.

The final chapter comprises a compendium of personal 'Commentaries' by professional individuals involved in observing the progress of COVID-19 since 2020. These 'personal reflections' are wide-ranging in their content, providing contrasting overviews of the pandemic and enabling the reader to make up their own mind on the British government's response to the pandemic.

Chapter One: Early Beginnings

The Coronavirus

The name Coronavirus derives from the Latin 'corona' meaning 'crown' or 'wreath', which describes the characteristic surface spikes on the virus which resemble a 'halo'. This particular virus was first discovered in the 1930s due to an outbreak of respiratory infection discovered in domesticated chickens in China. An infectious 'bronchitis' virus caused this outbreak.

According to their specific characteristics, there are four main types of coronavirus; Alpha, Beta, Gamma and Delta. Whilst the majority of these four types only affect animals, there are a few that can also pass to humans. Those that transmit to humans belong to just two types, the Alpha and Beta.

Only two coronaviruses have previously caused global outbreaks. The first was the SARS coronavirus responsible for 'severe acute respiratory syndrome', hence the title SARS-CoV. SARS first started spreading in China in 2002 and primarily affected the populations of mainland China and Hong Kong before fading out in 2003. The other virus was the MERS-CoV coronavirus or 'Middle-East Respiratory Syndrome', emerging in Saudi Arabia in 2012. The estimated fatality rate for SARS was between 14 and 15% of the confirmed cases. MERS had a fatality rate of around 35%.

In contrast, coronaviruses do vary significantly in terms of their risk factors. Human coronaviruses were identified and classified in the 1960s, and to date, they are:

SARS-CoV	2003
HCoV-NL63	2004
HcoV-HK-V1	2005
MERS-CoV	2012
SARS-CoV-2 (COVID-19)	2019-20

Some coronaviruses kill more than 30% of those infected – such as the MERS-CoV. Others are relatively harmless, for example, the 'common cold'. However, these can cause major symptoms such as fever and sore throat. They can also cause pneumonia either directly, as in 'viral pneumonia' or by 'secondary bacterial infection' and bronchitis.

Such viruses cause about 15% of common colds in adults and children, but between 40 and 50% of colds are caused by 'rhinoviruses'. These rhinoviruses produce the familiar inflammation of the mucous membranes of the nose (acute rhinitis), together with the throat and bronchial tubes.

In December 2019, a pneumonia outbreak was reported in Wuhan Province, China, and was identified as a 'novel' variant of coronavirus and named 'SARS-CoV-2'. This Wuhan strain was identified as a 'new' variant of Beta-Coronavirus with approximately 79% genetic similarity to bat coronavirus (bat-CoV-2C45 and bat-SL-CoV-ZXC21).

It is widely suspected to have originated from bat populations because its genomic sequence is 88% that of the bat coronavirus. This virus's DNA is approximately 50% similar to that of the MERS-CoV virus. In effect, SARS-CoV2 or COVID-19 is a combination of three coronaviruses; SARS-CoV, the bat coronavirus and MERS-CoV.

SARS emerged in 2003 in Asia before developing rapidly globally. This outbreak resulted in more than 8,000 confirmed infections, 10% of which proved fatal. In

September 2012, a new strain of coronavirus was identified but did not appear to transmit readily from human-to-human. This strain was the MERS virus. Then in May 2013, a case of human-to-human transmission was detected in France, but with a limited number of infection cases.

By October 2013, another 124 cases of MERS were detected in Saudi Arabia, resulting in 52 deaths – approximately 42% of the total confirmed cases. Then in May 2015, a further outbreak of MERS-CoV occurred in Korea. By December 2015, this outbreak had expanded to become the largest outbreak in the Middle East. There were approximately 2,468 confirmed cases of infection, together with a mortality rate of between 34 and 35%.

SARS was a coronavirus originating in Beijing, China, between November 2002 and July 2003, before spreading to over 26 countries worldwide. This outbreak resulted in 8,096 cases of infection and 774 deaths, with a fatality rate of approximately 9.6%. SARS ended up infecting 5,237 people in mainland China alone.

The current COVID-19 overtook SARS in January 2020, when Chinese officials confirmed 5,974 cases of what we now recognise as COVID-19. By the close of January 2020, the virus had resulted in approximately 8,096 cases of infection globally, which by 5 July 2020 had increased to 11,125,245 confirmed global cases. By this date, there were recorded a total of 528,204 deaths, giving a fatality rate of approximately 4.8%.

The Origin of COVID-19 and Conspiracy Theories

"In June 2020, a former MI6 Director-General, Sir Richard Dearlove, was accused by the British Government of peddling fanciful claims that coronavirus was accidentally created in a Chinese laboratory. British security agencies believed COVID-19 was not a man-made virus and that it was highly likely to have occurred naturally, and spread to humans via animal hosts. However, Sir Richard, who was head of MI6 from 1999 to 2004, drew attention to a report which claimed that the virus was 'accidentally manufactured by Chinese scientists'. In support of his theory, Sir Richard claimed that the Beijing leadership has attempted to stifle any public debate regarding the resultant pandemic, which involved people being arrested and silenced. The report Sir Richard referred to was written by Professor Angus Dalgleish from St George's Hospital, London, and a Norwegian virologist Birger Sorensen. This report claims that the virus was manufactured in a laboratory, and was contributing to the ongoing debate about how the virus first evolved and broke out, resulting in the 'pandemic'. The study claimed to have identified 'inserted sections' on the surface of the COVID-19 viruses surface, that were significantly different to any other similar virus studied to date.

The British Government's view was that there is no evidence to substantiate that the virus is 'man-made'. World leading scientists in the UK, the US and the World Health Organisation (WHO) have repeatedly stated that the virus was 'natural in origin', and became transmitted into the human population through 'natural transfer' from animal sources. Consequently, it was not the result of a specific accident or man-made accident."

Source: "Spy Chief in Virus Storm", Daily Mail, 5 June 2020 page 12. Author: Larisa Brown, Defence and Security Editor.

"Sir Richard's claim was subject to an in-depth Analysis which clarified the issues raised by Sir Richard and placed these within the correct context of events. In April, 2020, an investigative documentary entitled *Tracking Down the Origin of the Wuhan Coronavirus* was released on-line. It claimed 'conclusive proof' that the COVID-19 virus had been created as a biological weapon of mass destruction in a Chinese laboratory. On behalf of the *Daily Mail*, journalist John Naish carried out a comprehensive check on the experts involved and the factual evidence presented in the documentary.

This involved contacting some of the world's best independent scientific authorities for their opinion. There was unanimous consensus that Sir Richard's concerns did not stand up to scrutiny. The April documentary had in fact, been produced by a US-based anti-Chinese government organisation, the Epoch Times. It appears that the documentary's 'experts' were in reality 'hard-Rightists'. At the same time, rumours emerged that a 'sensational, piece of biological science by both British and Norwegian investigators was due to be published in a reputable journal. It appears that experts who were sent the paper for 'peer review' were astounded by the claim that it had established 'beyond reasonable doubt' that COVID-19 was an 'engineered virus'. The authors alleged the COVID-19 virus had 'unique fingerprints' that could not have evolved naturally. They were, therefore, indicative of 'purposive manipulation'... The paper concluded that COVID-19 should correctly be called the 'Wuhan Virus'.

The initial paper to which Sir Richard Dearlove referred, failed stringent tests of verification and is understood to have been rejected in April by eminent international journals such as *Nature* and the *Journal of Virology*. After successive re-writes, the paper was published by the *Quarterly Review of Biophysics Discovery* in June 2020. Significantly, no accusations of Chinese manipulation appear in this final paper. This re-written paper describes the virus as a 'Chimera', meaning that it contains the viral genetic material of more than one virus. This can occur naturally when two viruses infect a living creature at the same time. This is the reason that leading experts believe that the COVID-19 virus acquired its 'pandemic' powers through 'jumping between species'. However, another definition of a 'Chimera' virus is one that has been created in a laboratory as a 'bio-weapon', but the paper only vaguely implies foul play.

In conclusion, the authors of the original paper are demanding to know where COVID-19 came from, as indeed, is the watching world. It cannot be denied that the Chinese authorities have done plenty to arouse suspicion about the virus's origin. They also have 'form' when it comes to poor biosecurity. They let a lethal SARS virus escape from a Beijing laboratory in April 2004. This infected nine people before the outbreak was contained. Despite this, the overwhelming consensus is COVID-19 originated in nature, and most likely infected us through trade in live animals for food."
Source: "Wild Theories That Didn't Stand Up To Scrutiny". Analysis by John Naish, Daily Mail, 5 June 2020, page 12.

"Secrets, lies and thuggery are the hallmark of the Chinese Communist regime, and in the mystery of the devastating Wuhan virus, all three are combined. The strongest evidence of a crime is a cover-up, and the Chinese authorities have provided that. They have fought ferociously to prevent an international inquiry into the origin of the pandemic. Their repeated obstruction of the World Health Organisation's (WHO) fact-finding missions have provoked protest. Even now, WHO investigators are being prevented from accessing the vitally important laboratory in Wuhan that is likely to be at the heart of America's allegations. Experts have been questioning the Chinese authorities' account of events for a year. Now it appears Secretary of

State Mike Pompeo is to make a direct accusation. Was it really pure chance the virus first attacked the human race in the only city in China with a research laboratory specialising in manipulating the world's most dangerous viruses? That would be as odd as a new disease emerging in the surroundings of Britain's top-secret biological defence research establishment at Porton Down in Wiltshire. To this day, scientists who support the theory that the virus is a mutation that emerged from Wuhan's 'wet market', have not been able to find a convincing candidate for the animal in which this mutation is believed to have actually occurred.

The 'official' explanation is the new virus was 96 per cent identical to a bat virus, RaTG13, found in Yunnan Province in Southern China. But as Chinese professor Botao Xiao pointed out in a paper published in February, no such bats are sold at the city's markets. The caves where they live are hundreds of miles away. That paper disappeared from the Internet, and professor Xiao, perhaps mindful of the fate that awaits those in China who promote 'inconvenient truth', disavowed it. Many scientists privately assumed an engineered virus released via a laboratory accident was at least as likely as the idea of a series of stunningly unfortunate 'chance mutations'. After all, Dr Shi Zhengli, the Chinese scientist nicknamed 'Bat Woman', was a regular visitor to the caves in Yunnan Province. When news of the outbreak broke, she initially feared that a leak from her research institute was to blame. That thought alone should have prompted a full-scale and searching inquiry. Instead, the Chinese Ministry of Education issued a diktat: "Any paper that traces the origin of the virus must be strictly and tightly managed". But even the Chinese regime cannot hold back the truth forever. Over the past twelve months, independent research, official leaks, and news reports have strengthened the 'lab-leak' hypothesis. In February, 2021, a Taiwanese professor, Fang Chi-tai, highlighted a curious feature of the virus's genetic code, which would make it more effective in attacking targeted cells. This was unlikely to be the result of a 'natural mutation' he suggested.

Much scientific research involves modifying viruses to understand how they function. Many observers have worried for years that the risks of such experiments are not properly thought through. Laboratory safety procedures are riddled with potential loopholes and flaws; breakages, animal bites, faulty equipment or sample mislabelling can all lead to a deadly pathogen reaching its first human victim. If so, such carelessness has now cost tens of millions of lives. Yet we should be clear, the Chinese authorities are ruthless. But even they would not unleash a global Plague. Only in the fevered imagination of conspiracy theorists is Beijing deliberately waging biological warfare on the West. Paradoxically, such speculation is promoted by among others, President Donald Trump's former adviser, Steve Bannon, who may have hampered the search for the truth by making the lab-release theory seem racist and politically toxic. In February 2021, in Britain's politically correct media field, *The Lancet*, scientists published an open-letter denouncing conspiracy theories and rumours, urging solidarity with Chinese colleagues. Yet, it was just those colleagues who were bearing the brunt of the regime's frantic attempts to censor the truth about the outbreak. The Chinese regime prizes self-preservation above all, certainly, over the truth, or the health of its own people, let alone the lives of foreigners".

Source: Commentary, Daily Mail, 13 January 2021, page 8. Author: Edward Lucas.

"It is 'feasible' that the COVID-19 global pandemic originated in a Chinese research facility, the UK's Secret Intelligence Service MI6, now believes. Previously, MI6 thought there was only a 'remote' chance that the leak came from a laboratory in Wuhan. But spy chiefs have now reached a different conclusion. Sources reportedly said the theory was 'feasible' and it comes as Britain said the World Health Organisation (WHO) must be allowed by China to conduct an 'unencumbered' investigation. The WHO yesterday (30 May) also altered its position on the origin of the virus, having previously suggested it was extremely unlikely to have spread from a laboratory source. Director-General Dr Tedros Ghebreyesus now said that all hypotheses about the origin of the virus 'remain on the table'. He also described the WHO's initial probe as 'not extensive enough' and called for further investigations. The WHO's determination to dig deeper into the source of the virus, which has caused more than 3.5 million deaths worldwide, was backed by Britain's vaccines minister Nadhim Zahawi; "The WHO at every step of the way has tried to share as much data with the world, as it is able to verify", he said. "This is a very difficult situation, and it is only right the WHO is allowed to conduct its investigation unencumbered, into the origin of the pandemic."

Beijing continues to deny that the global crisis began with a leak from a laboratory in Wuhan. Controversy is also growing over the alleged silencing of Chinese scientists who wanted an investigation into the 'lab-leak' theory. Tom Tugendhat, Chairman of the Government's foreign affairs committee said, "The silence coming from Wuhan is troubling. We need to open the crypt and see what happened to be able to protect ourselves in the future". Sources told the *Sunday Times* that British intelligence agencies now think it is possible that the lab-leak theory is true. It comes as US President Joe Biden has ordered his intelligence officials to 'redouble' their efforts to investigate the origins of the pandemic, including the option that it was 'man-made'. He has given the CIA and other agencies 90 days to complete their findings and pledged to release their results to the public.

In June, 2020, the *Quarterly Review of Biophysics*

Discovery published the paper by Professor Angus Dalgleish and Dr Birger Sorensen which claimed COVID-19 has 'no credible natural ancestor'. Dr Dalgleish, a professor of oncology at St George's University Hospital, London, said; "Scientists then 'retro-engineered' the virus they had created to make out it was in a sequence years ago. The virus leaked from the Wuhan Institute of Virology because of poor biosecurity."
Source: "Pressure on Beijing as MI6 Adds Weight to Lab-Leak Theory" Daily Mail, 31 May 2021, page 10. Authors: Mark Nicol and Colin Fernandez.

"There is compelling scientific evidence the coronavirus leaked from a Chinese laboratory two US experts say; It has a genetic sequence which has 'never been found naturally' in the same class of coronavirus, and instead is usually only found when scientists try to 'intentionally supercharge' a virus in a lab. The researchers suggest the CGG-CGG sequence used to make protein rarely appears naturally when viruses mutate as there are 35 other similar sequences which are more likely to develop. They also added that it was the "sequence of choice" in labs, because it is convenient, and scientists have experience of inserting it into viruses. Writing in the *Wall Street Journal*, Dr Steven Quay, previously of Stanford University, and Professor Richard Muller of the University of California, said; "This fact that the coronavirus with all its random possibilities, took the rare and unnatural combination used by human researchers, implies that the leading theory for the origin of the coronavirus must be 'laboratory escape'."
Source: Daily Mail, 8 June 2021, page 8. Author: Victoria Allen, Science Correspondent.

The Progress Of COVID-19 In England

The COVID-19 pandemic was first confirmed to have spread to England with two cases of Chinese nationals staying in York on 31 January 2020. By the end of that month, it was estimated that approximately 22% of the population of the country had contracted the coronavirus. By 6 February 2020, a third confirmed case was reported in Brighton, and by 10 February, the total number of cases in England had reached eight. All were linked to the Brighton case.

On the same day, the Secretary for Health and Social Care, Matt Hancock, announced the implementation of the Health Protection (Coronavirus) Regulations 2020. These regulations gave public health professionals powers to keep affected persons in isolation. On 11 February, a ninth case was confirmed in London. By 1 March, further cases were reported in areas of Greater Manchester in the North-West of the country. On the following day, four more people in England tested positive. All had recently travelled from Italy.

By this point, the total number of English cases had reached 40, and within two days, the number of confirmed cases had risen to 51. On 2 March, the first coronavirus death occurred in a care home, and on the following day, the first three hospital deaths were announced in Nottingham, Essex and Buckinghamshire.

By 17 March, NHS England announced that all non-urgent operations would be postponed from 15 April to free up 30,000 beds. Many affected patients were discharged into care homes, but few of these were tested for COVID 19. This serious overlook resulted in the spread of the virus into many care homes in England. On the same day, the Chancellor of the Exchequer, Rishi Sunak, announced that £300 billion would be made available in loan guarantees for businesses affected by the pandemic. By 18 March, more than 1,000 patients were hospitalised with COVID-19 in England, and by the end of March, confirmed cases stood at 21,000. This made England the worst affected country in the UK. During March, approximately 4,500 deaths occurred in hospitals, over 200 deaths in care homes, and another 200 deaths at home. On 2 April, the maximum number of hospitalisations in one day during the first wave of the pandemic reached approximately 3,000 patients, with daily hospital deaths running in excess of 600. By 12 April, the number of patients in hospital peaked at 18,974, whilst the number of daily admissions fell below 1,900. However, hospital deaths increased to more than 700. On 29 April, the total deaths reported by NHS England stood at 21,400. However, the number of patients hospitalised with COVID-19 showed a steady decline, and by 30 April, this stood at approximately 12,900.

During April 2020, around 54,100 patients had been admitted to hospital with COVID, and the number of deaths exceeded 17,500. By 3 May, the daily hospital admissions decreased to around 1,000, with 10,500 total admissions. On 12 May, the number of people hospitalised fell below 10,000, but the total hospital deaths had unfortunately increased since the beginning of March to approximately 24,500. On 21 May, the number of patients hospitalised had fallen below 8,000, with daily admission at around 700.

The 'lock-down' rules first implemented in March were amended in England to allow people to meet one other person from another household 'outdoors' but to remain at the social distance of 2 metres. Outdoor sports were allowed with members of the same household or one from another household while still maintaining social distancing rules. Households were allowed to drive any distance in England to a destination but not to Wales or Scotland.

The number of patients in hospital with COVID-19 continued to fall until 31 May, when it stood at around

5,900. During May, 22,400 patients had been admitted to hospital, of which around 5,200 died. It was concluded that travel from Italy resulted in most importations of the virus into England in mid-to-late February. However, by 1 March, this had changed to Spain, and by mid-March, it changed again to France. As a result of the government's travel restrictions being imposed on these three countries, importation of the virus was at very low levels. It was estimated that around 50% of the importations of COVID-19 were a direct result of UK nationals returning from these three countries. In the period up to early May 2020, approximately 34% of detected transmission lineages had arrived in England via Spain, 29% from France and 23% from other countries. By 15 June, hospitalisations had fallen to around 3,900, with daily admissions running at about 360. However, daily deaths were still at about 50.

On 30 June, the government imposed the first 'local lock-down' after 10% of all positive COVID cases over the previous seven days were located within the city of Leicester. As a result, non-essential shops in the city had to close, pubs and restaurants had to delay opening for at least two weeks, and schools closed for most pupils. However, by the end of June, the daily COVID hospital admissions were less than 200, with deaths at 30. At the end of June, the total number of hospital deaths was less than 2,700. From 24 July,

Government regulations made it compulsory to wear face coverings in most indoor venues such as shops, banks, post offices and on all forms of public transport.

Those members of the public breaching the rules faced fines of up to £100, but face coverings remained optional in indoor public places such as nurseries, cinemas and hairdressers. Exemptions were also available for children under the age of one and those individuals with physical or mental illness or disability. Throughout July 2020, the total number of COVID hospital admissions fell to around 3,500 and hospital deaths at around 480. August saw the lowest monthly hospital admissions since the start of the pandemic, at approximately 1,600, with hospital deaths at 208. The total number of patients in hospital at the end of August was under 500. On 15 August, the rules aimed at curtailing the spread of COVID-19 were eased. At the beginning of September, the minimum number of hospital patients since the start of the pandemic was recorded at 451, and hospital admissions were down to around 60 per day. Deaths in hospitals were around 40 per day by the end of the month.

However, on 8 September, following a significant increase in the number of reported cases, the government published new social distancing rules, which came into force in England from 14 September. These restricted gatherings of separate households to groups of six or fewer people (Rule of Six), excluding educational settings. By 18 September, the value of the 'R' number in England was now estimated to be 1.4. This meant that cases of coronavirus were doubling every seven days. At the end of September, hospital admissions for COVID had increased to around 5,900, with 560 hospital deaths. Between July and September 2020, more extensive and increasingly 'ad hoc' local regulations were introduced. However, in many areas of England, these interventions proved unsuccessful in controlling the spread of the virus.

On 14 October, all of these 'local' regulations in England were replaced by a new Tier System of regulations with three levels of restrictions. However, with the easing of restrictions and the arrival of a second more infectious variant of COVID-19, a second wave of the virus became well established in England by the end of October 2020. Hospital admissions saw a rapid increase from less than 6,000 in September to well over 25,000 in October. Almost 3,500 patients died in hospital. Following further forecasts predicting unsustainable pressure on the healthcare system, new uniform national restrictions were put into place from 5 November to at least 2 December 2020. Despite these tighter regulations, the number of hospital admissions during November increased to more than 41,200 and hospital deaths around 8,300. By 30 November, there were a total of 13,700 patients in hospital. In London alone, the new coronavirus variant accounted for around 25% of the total cases.

From 2 December, the national restrictions were replaced by the second version of Tier regulations with three levels of severity, according to the prevalence of infections. 57% of areas in the country were placed in 'Tier 2' and 42% in the highest 'Tier 3'. The government also announced that from the 23rd to 27th December 2020, a 'Christmas Bubble' would be permitted. This would allow people from up to three households to meet in private homes or gardens, but not 'indoors'. They were also permitted to travel between 'Tiers' to meet others in the same 'bubble'. After the appearance of the new variant coronavirus, referred to as Variant of Concern 202012/01, the government issued a new public health guide and were expected to impose travel restrictions. By mid-December, around two-thirds of the new cases were reported in London. On 19 December, it was announced that a new 'Tier Four' measure would be applied to London, Kent, Essex, Bedfordshire, Buckinghamshire and Hertfordshire. Consequently, Christmas season relaxation would be limited to Christmas Day only.

However, these attempts at controlling the second wave had only limited success. During December, hospital admissions rose to more than 58,600, with deaths in hospitals approaching 10,600. By the end of 2020, there were still more than 22,700 patients hospitalised. In January 2021, a 'third lock-down' in England was announced, with similar rules being enforced to the first lock-down in March 2020. Schools were to close for most pupils from 5 January. A 'peak' in hospital admissions occurred on 12 January with 4,134 patients, and by 18 January, the number of people already in hospitals stood at 34,336. This number was 80% higher than in the 'first wave' of March 2020.

In January, the total number of patients admitted to hospital with COVID-19 exceeded 100,000, and 22,000 deaths were recorded. On 1 February, door-to-door testing was announced by the government to identify cases of a new South African variant of coronavirus. There were around 80,000 tests carried out across eight different areas of the country. Eleven cases were identified in which the people had 'no recent travel history'. By the end of February, the daily reported cases fell as low as they were during September 2020, with 5,080 cases reported in England on 28 February. In February, more than 35,800 people had been admitted to hospital, of which 9,400 had died. On 3 March, it was reported that less than 10,000 patients were in hospital for the first time since the beginning of November 2020. On 8 March, students returned to face-to-face teaching in schools and colleges, with rapid testing being carried out in secondary schools.

By 13 March, more than 20 million UK residents had received their first dose of a COVID-19 vaccine, and over 1 million had received their second dose. On 29 March, the next phase of easing the national lock-down took place. People were able to meet up in groups of six or as two households outdoors, and sporting facilities could re-open. Cases declined towards the end of March, with less than 3,000 infections being recorded per day. On 5 April, the next phase of the lock-down was announced with non-essential shops re-opening from 12 April, and pubs were allowed to open but only 'outdoors'. Over 10 million people had been fully vaccinated by 23 April.

COVID Regulations and Legislation in England

The government published the Health Protection (Coronavirus) Regulations 2020 on 10 February 2020. This was a Statutory Instrument covering the legal framework behind the government's initial containment and isolation strategy and its organisation of the national reaction to the virus in England.

On 19 March 2020, the government introduced the Coronavirus Act 2020, which granted the government 'discretionary emergency powers' in the area of the NHS, social care, schools, policing, the Border Force, local councils and courts of law. This Act received Royal Assent on 25 March 2020.

The closure of pubs, restaurants and all indoor sports facilities was permitted by the Health Protection (Coronavirus Business Closure) England, Regulations. 2020. In England, until 14 October 2020, most of the COVID-19 'lock-down' regulations covered the whole of the country. However, some local areas of particular concern were also subject to more restrictive rules at variable times.

In England, the local 'lock-down' regulations were abolished on 14 October to be replaced by the First COVID-19 Tier Regulations. These were to be Three Tiers ranging from medium to high and very high. These were referred to as the First Tier Regulations.

Following the November lock-down, a new framework of 'Tiers' known as Second Tier Regulations were introduced, and these applied from 2 December 2020 until February 2021. Also, in December 2020, a new Fourth Tier was added to the Second Tier Regulations.

Households in this tier were subjected to further restraints, including a travel ban 'outside' their specific area, a ban on international travel, and meeting more than one person outside. In March 2020, to enforce these regulations, police forces in England were given powers to arrest and fine citizens who broke lock-down rules. The National Police Chief's Council stated that police had issued their first fines on 27 March 2020. The fixed penalty notices were £60 but would be reduced to £30 if paid within 14 days of issue.

According to police data, around 9,000 people were issued notices between 27 March and 27 April. Figures for 27 March to 11 May 2020 showed that more than 14,000 fines were issued, with 862 repeat offenders, one person having been fined nine times. The Easter weekend of 11-12th April 2020 saw the highest number of fines issued.

Reports were also made of 'hate' incidents against Italian and Chinese people, linked to the coronavirus 'public fear'.

The outcome of COVID-19 has had a detrimental effect on global healthcare systems and virtually every aspect of human life as we know it.

The World Health Organisation (WHO) declared the COVID-19 outbreak a 'global pandemic' on 30 January 2020. In response to flattening the curve of infections, governments enforced barrier and quarantine measures in the countries that constituted the world's largest economies. Not unexpectedly, these actions sparked fears of an impending economic and social crisis. It is to examine the socio-economic impact of the pandemic in England that we now turn in Chapter Two.

Chapter Two: The Socio-Economic Impact of COVID-19 in England

Health and Social Care

The coronavirus pandemic and the government's measures to control the spread of the virus have deeply affected our lives: people's income, employment, security and social interactions. Such factors are vital to leading healthy and fulfilled lives.

Together with the local government, the NHS workforce has restructured their work to contain the infection and protect the most vulnerable. However, this has been undertaken against the reality of successive years of budget reductions. The NHS responded to the acute requirements of COVID-19 while also delivering 'scaled back' non-COVID health care. In particular, social care has been weakened by years of reduced public financing and rising demand and therefore has been left reeling from the impact of the virus.

Early evidence from China and subsequently Italy suggested that the virus was more likely to kill older people who had underlying medical conditions and were predominantly male. However, underlying conditions are not easily distributed across the population of England - they are more common in deprived communities.

The 'indirect' impact on people with acute conditions that are not COVID-19 related is of particular concern. In March 2020, NHS Trusts in England re-designed their services on a large scale to release extra capacity to treat COVID patients. This re-design included discharging thousands of patients to free up beds, postponing planned elective treatment, moving appointments online and re-deploying staff. By April, concerns were being raised about the significant drops in Accident and Emergency use and admissions for urgent conditions. These included such serious conditions as stroke and heart attacks. The full impact of the significant reduction in 'routine' NHS care in England has not been fully acknowledged.

The 'hidden' impact of the COVID crisis is the serious compromise of patient safety. Millions of patients living with health problems, including life-threatening conditions such as cancer, have been affected, with their treatment postponed or cancelled. This is not just the result of the virus itself but the knock-on effects of an unprecedented disruption to vital NHS services.

Although a pandemic on the scale of COVID-19 was inevitably going to cause major disruption to health services in England, the drastic extent to which the NHS had to shut down routine care is a direct consequence of over a decade's under-investment and cuts to health services.

As a result, NHS capacity has lagged behind many other European countries regarding bed numbers, critical care facilities and workforce numbers. In 2019 there were 10,000 medical vacancies in the NHS. More than 3.5 million patients over 50 had operations or treatment on the NHS cancelled during the first 'lock-down' in 2020. Almost a quarter of those needing to see their GP said they could not do so. Three out of four needing community health and social care, including dentists, counsellors or personal carers, went without during the COVID peak.

A report published by the Institute for Fiscal Studies in 2020 painted a bleak picture of routine health care during the first wave, just as England entered a second national lock-down. Patient groups said the report's findings supported the 'chilling statistics' of a sharp rise in older people dying in their own homes. They warned that the country's health could not afford for such widespread disruption to happen again, with more than four million already on the NHS waiting list.

The report found that a sixth of the over 50s population in England (some 3.6 million people) had some hospital treatment cancelled between February and May 2020. One in seven of those who reported needing a GP, and more than a third wanting community care, did not even attempt to contact these services. This would suggest that they were either frightened of becoming infected with the virus or did not wish to be a burden on the system. This report came out as the country started a second lock-down following a resurgence in virus cases. The report concluded that "as we move into another lock-down, it will be crucial to ensure access to routine care is maintained as much as possible, and a plan is in place to address backlogs built up in the first few months of the pandemic. Without this commitment, we risk entrenching existing health inequalities for years to come".

According to a study by the British Medical Journal (BMJ), cancer patients' risk of dying increases by up to 10% for every month their treatment is delayed. This report lays bare how the devastating disruption to cancer services during the pandemic will cost thousands of lives. Research reveals that around 33,000 cancer patients in the UK faced delays in starting treatment. The BMJ, using data for 1.2 million patients worldwide, found that postponing treatment by just one month raises the risk of death by around 10%. Survival chances deteriorate the longer that treatments are postponed. The BMJ study found there is no 'safe' amount of time for which treatment can be postponed. It is essential to start therapy as soon as possible after the initial diagnosis.

The Lethal Impact of 'Lockdowns' on the Nation's Health

The damage inflicted by 'lock-downs' extends into every sphere of health, including cancer, heart disease, addiction, the welfare of children, domestic violence and mental illness. Even after the pandemic ends, it will take years for the NHS to catch up with backlogs. This will be too late for tens of thousands of patients.

Both doctors and politicians called on the government to ensure all health services were protected if the spread of COVID-19 continues. Delays in treatment will cause a 20% rise in deaths among newly diagnosed cancer patients in England. Treatment for strokes fell by 45% during lock-down, and there were more than 2,000 excess deaths from heart disease. More than 50,000 operations for children were cancelled. Organ transplants fell by two-thirds, with the number of those who died on the waiting list almost doubling. Waiting lists for routine orthopaedic and eye operations are at record levels. Calls received by child abuse helplines have rocketed. As rates of depression and anxiety doubled, thousands of recovering alcoholics relapsed. At least 25,000 more people have died at home during the pandemic. This was because they were either unable or chose not to go to hospital, a surge of 43.8% on normal levels.

Over 85,400 people died in private homes rather than in hospitals or care homes between 20 March, when the first lock-down began, and 11 September 2020. This was the equivalent of around 100 excess deaths per day. The Office for National Statistics (ONS) found that rates of depression across all ages and genders in England roughly doubled from one in ten to one in five. A paper in the *British Journal of Psychiatry* stated that 18% of UK adults reported having suicidal thoughts in the first month of the lock-down. Another suggested that there was a high probability that suicides would increase.

Leading mental health experts have warned that lock-downs would trigger spikes of suicide, self-harm, alcoholism and domestic abuse. One consultant psychologist remarked that a lock-down is supposed to prevent deaths from COVID but is also certain to cause further deaths, not only from other physical diseases but from alcoholism, addiction and suicide. Lock-downs also lead to intense loneliness and depression, and in older people, these are killers and closely linked to poor physical health, leaving them more vulnerable to COVID. Social connections and human touch are essential for psychological stability. Isolation can lead to loneliness and is a predictor of suicidal thoughts.

Britain has been harder hit by the coronavirus pandemic because the NHS is under-resourced and under-staffed. It took the UK twenty days longer than the whole of Europe to bring the first wave of the virus under control during the spring of 2020. The understaffing argument was expressed in a report published by the Organisation for Economic Cooperation and Development. One important function of this organisation is to monitor health provision and patient outcomes across the EU. The report states that it took 54 days for the UK to reduce the 'R' rate to less than one for four consecutive days. Only Sweden took longer at 58 days, the European average being 34 days. It was NHS staff problems that caused the most constraint on England's response to the first wave of the pandemic. This, together with a lack of contact training capacity, constrained the UK's ability to deal with the virus outbreak effectively.

"Operation Moonshot, the British Government's flagship testing programme, whose aim was to test the entire population for COVID-19, failed miserably. Four experts from the universities of Bristol, Warwick, Newcastle and Birmingham warned that the rapid tests used for the programme, set to cost taxpayers billions of pounds, had not been properly discussed for their accuracy. They stated the proposals, which were already being piloted in Liverpool, had been developed without the agreement of the UK National Screening Committee. This is the body responsible for advising Government on appropriate screening strategy. The experts warned that getting 'inaccurate' negative results could offer false reassurance to the public, thereby encouraging 'risky' behaviour and spreading the virus rather than containing it.

Professor John Deeks of Birmingham University said the concept of 'test and release' when someone is allowed to return to 'normal' life after a negative result was inherently 'dangerous'. The arguments that this test can tell the difference between infections and non-infections are not substantiated by any data. In addition, false positives will force people to self-isolate unnecessarily. Professor Deeks said if all 68 million people in the country were to be tested, there would be at least 400,000 who would be incorrectly told that they were carrying the virus. He further added that the test would only pick up when an individual was at their most infectious. Even if those problems were ironed out, society-wide screening will cost more than any other healthcare intervention contemplated, and has the potential to cause harm through significant division of resources. It may cost up to £100 billion.

Dr Angela Raffle, consultant in public health and honorary senior lecturer at the University of Bristol, said: "Moonshot seemed to me to be the most unethical proposal for use of public funds or for screening that I have ever seen". The experts said that 'population' screening for COVID has not been endorsed by the WHO or the SAGE advisory body".

Source: "Moonshot Tests Drive Doomed", Daily Mail, 17 November 2020, Page 14. Author: Ben Spencer, Medical Correspondent.

Research indicates that the number of adults suffering from depression has more than doubled since the pandemic. According to scientists, more than one in five people in England showed signs of depression during the first three months of 2020. Women were worst hit as four in ten under-30s were classed as depressed. The figure for men in the same age group was 26%.

The Office for National Statistics (ONS) released two ground-breaking studies. The finding that one in five people were suffering from depression was drawn from routine ONS Surveys, while the conclusion that more patients were asking for help in England was drawn from GP records. Twenty-five thousand people were asked if they were feeling depressed, took no interest or pleasure in life, slept too little or too much, ate too little or too much, lost concentration, were haunted by feelings of failure or were worried about letting down their families. These were classed as depressed.

Between late January and early March 2021, 21% of British adults were experiencing depression. This figure was 10% before the pandemic and 19% when the second lock-down began in November 2020. When looking at adults on low incomes, or those who had been hit hard economically by the lock-down, one in three had suffered mental health issues. Issues were worse among the young (the age group most likely affected by school closures). Research also found that 43% of women under 30, and 26% of men of the same age group, were depressed.

It has been revealed by research carried out by Imperial College, London, that COVID-19 could age the brain by at least ten years or cause IQ to fall. Researchers have pointed out that those who suffered worse from the virus could inherit lasting mental damage equivalent to an IQ drop of 8.5 (or the brain ageing by up to ten years). A symptom named 'brain fog' has been reported by 'long-term' COVID sufferers after their initial post-viral recovery. The fog included symptoms such as loss of memory and the inability to hold a conversation. According to scientists, this is a sign of 'chronic cognitive consequences'.

These findings came from analysing questionnaire answers from around 85,000 participants who had recovered from confirmed or suspected COVID-19. Damage to the brain varied depending on the severity of the disease. Some patients who had been treated in intensive care or on ventilators recorded an 8.5 point drop in their IQ. Those who recovered at home also experienced an IQ drop of four points, the equivalent of ageing by five years.

The researchers also found that COVID survivors scored poorly on 'spatial orientation, emotion processing, and maintaining attention' tests. They were able to compare the test results to pre-COVID times because the 85,000 people sampled had previously answered questions as part of the Great British Intelligence Test. These answers provided a benchmark for IQ before the onset of the COVID-19 pandemic.

A Cynical and Brazen Cronyism

"The mismanagement, the incompetence, the reckless waste, all of this is shocking. But worse, perhaps, is the brazen cronyism involved. The *National Audit Office Report on Personal Protective Equipment* (PPE), is a searing indictment of this government's incompetence. Yes, there was an unprecedented crisis. As the virus rampaged through hospitals and care homes, there was a desperate shortage of PPE. Understandably the government made a dramatic appeal to suppliers, please get in touch, we need you. But it awarded PPE contracts worth billions to companies not on the basis of quality or price, but in many cases, according to today's damning report, on which firms had the best personal contacts in Westminster and Whitehall. This isn't how public procurement in Britain is meant to work. Strict, legally binding rules are supposed to enforce fairness and transparency, promote competitive pricing, and to prevent conflict of interest.

But thanks to the pandemic, the report suggests: "the rules were cast aside, and replaced in many cases by the 'old pals act'". The report confirms what this newspaper revealed two weeks ago, that well-connected firms and individuals could be put on a 'VIP Route' officially called a 'high priority lane', meaning decisions on their potential contracts were fast-tracked. Once recommended, these firms were more than ten times as likely to win contracts. The result is we have been landed with equipment that has often turned out to be useless, and with bills that are far higher than they should have been. At the same time, those with real expertise and the ability to produce quality products at a good price have been sidelined.

Take Jonathan Bennett. As the Mail reported this month, he is a veteran textile importer with extensive contacts in China, where most PPE is made. His bid to supply millions of masks in April was highly competitive and well below the Government's 'bench mark' price. But the £253 million contract went to Ayanda Capital, a firm with no experience in the field which charged almost twice as much. Worse, 50 million of their masks were the wrong design. Mr Bennett has long suspected Ayanda won its contract because it was brokered by someone who until recently had been an adviser to the Trade Secretary, an Ayanda associate called Andrew Mills. The NAO Report confirms this. It was thanks to a 'referral' by Mr Mills that Ayanda's bid got the VIP treatment. Ayanda is far from the only company that benefited from fast-tracking, and went on to produce unsaleable PPE.

Each time the Department of Health is asked how these contracts were awarded, it says the same thing, that it always exercises strict 'due diligence'. Yet the NAO Report reveals that when department officials carried out 'due diligence' on Ayanda, they somehow failed to notice Mr Mill's involvement. So what were the criteria that determined who got VIP status? Amazingly, the NAO finds there were none, while the source of the referral for this treatment, "was not always recorded". In the Middle East, there is a term for this way of doing business: 'Wasta'. It means exploiting the access and influence someone has. Could this system really now be a feature of public policy in Britain? There are growing concerns over the allocation of up to £42 million on Operation Moonshot, a mass virus test-

ing. Insiders told me there has been a VIP channel in this process. Just how many more contracts will NAO investigators now find cause for concern over?"
Source: Daily Mail, 18th November 2020. Commentary by David Rose.

Social Care

"A report published by the Care Quality Commission (CQC) on 21 July, 2021, revealed that more than 39,000 care home residents were killed by COVID-19, over half of these deaths occurring in the first three months of the start of the pandemic. Some 152 care homes across England recorded deaths of at least 20 residents. Charities have described the numbers as 'heartbreaking' and 'devastating', and said they underscored the Government's 'tragic failures' to protect care homes. The figures show there were 39,265 deaths reported by homes between April 10 2020 and March 31 2021. This included 18,329 deaths recorded in the first three months of the pandemic, between April and the end of June last year.

Responding to the data, the Health Foundation said the Government's response had been 'too little, too late'. Former health secretary Matt Hancock had insisted in spring last year that officials had 'thrown a protective ring around our care homes' by giving them adequate support and resources. But his claims were quickly rebuffed by care home providers, who warned that thousands of residents were dying of the virus due to a lack of testing and insufficient personal protection equipment. The crisis was made worse as struggling hospitals discharged thousands of elderly patients into care homes without testing them in a rush to free up beds. Tragically, many of these patients had COVID and seeded outbreaks in the care homes which received them. The CQC's figures show that deaths of care home residents were significantly lower in the second wave, even tough overall case numbers were far higher, with 13,343 recorded between January and March 2021.

James White, head of public affairs and campaigns

at the Alzheimer's Society said; "At the start of the pandemic, we saw multiple failures impacting care homes. As COVID-19 spread in the local community, we saw a lack of protection for care homes, which is why we expressed significant concerns early on about hospital discharge into care homes, testing and PPE supplies. This heartbreaking new data shows the devastating and tragic consequences of those government failures". Hugh Alderwick, head of policy at the Health Foundation think-tank said: "...the data exposed the grim toll of the pandemic on care homes. Central Government support for social care during the pandemic was often too little, too late, particularly during the first wave".

Professor Martin Green, chief executive of Care England, the largest representative body of care providers said: "Care homes have been right at the front line of this dreadful pandemic. My thoughts go out to all those bereaved relatives as well as those dedicated staff who have been on high alert often working around the clock with no end in sight as well as all bereaved relatives. Every death is a tragedy and it would be highly disrespectful if lessons were not learned at every level". The figures show that care homes in the North West were hardest hit by the first wave, with 3,081 deaths recorded between April and June 2020. But it was the South East which was worst affected by the second wave, with 3,348 deaths between January and March 2021. The CQC pointed out that the residents did not necessarily catch COVID in their care homes. They might have been admitted to hospital with a broken hip for example, and contracted the virus on the ward. The CQC's figures refer to death notifications from care home managers after a resident has died from COVID-19. They are slightly different to the data from the Office for National Statistics which has reported approximately 42,000 care home deaths, covering an earlier time period and relating to information on death certificates.

Alongside the data on COVID death notifications, the CQC conducted 5,577 inspections of adult care providers between 10 April 2020 and 31 March 2021. The watchdog said that complaints, whistle-blowers and the absence of a registered manager were more likely to indicate poor care than death notifications. Kate Terroni, the CQC's chief inspector of adult social care, said: "We have a duty to be transparent, and to act in the public interest, and we made a commitment to publish data at this level, but only once we felt able to do so as accurately and safely as possible given the complexity and sensitivity of the data. In doing so, we aim to provide a more comprehensive picture of the impact of COVID-19 on care homes, the people living in them and their families. It is important to be clear, however, that although this data relates to deaths of people who were care home residents, many of them did not die in or contract COVID-19 in a care home".

A Department of Health and Social Care spokesman said: 'Throughout the pandemic we have done all we can to protect vulnerable people in adult social care. We have provided billions of pounds to support the sector, including on infection and prevention control measures, free PPE, priority vaccinations and additional testing'."
Source: Daily Mail, 22 July 2021, page 6. Author: Sophie Borland, Health Editor.

Thrown To The Wolves
"In spring last year, as coronavirus began wreaking carnage, then health secretary Matt Hancock boasted of casting a 'protective ring' around care homes. Today, a report reveals that, instead of being safeguarded by the State, vulnerable residents were thrown to the wolves. Calamitously slow to offer support, the government allowed those care homes to become houses of death. The Care Quality Commission reveals 39,000 residents died – many spending their final hours confused and alone. Blunders were myriad. Not only were staff denied protective clothing, they did not

receive crucial COVID tests. Most horrifying, NHS hospitals discharged infected patients back to nursing homes, triggering fatal outbreaks. This paper appreciates the government was straining every sinew to fight the virus and had constant demands on resources from every conceivable quarter. But in a civilised society, defending the vulnerable is an overriding moral duty. Tragically, those residents, mothers, fathers, grandparents, friends, were failed unforgivably."
Comment, Daily Mail, 22 July 2021, page 18.

"Just over two years ago, the NHS in England, outlined its strategic ambitions for the coming decade. At that point, no one could have anticipated the seismic shock the health and care system would soon face. It is now time to renew priorities in the light of this, embracing learning wherever it can be found, and seizing opportunities to create positive change for the longer term. The 2019 Conservative Party manifesto made the NHS a key priority, promised to solve the problems in social care to give every person the dignity and security that they deserve, and to 'level-up' every part of the country.

Making good on these commitments in the wake of the global COVID-19 pandemic, will require change and renewal, creating public services that can work hand in hand with local communities, solve the problems in social care to give every person the dignity and security that they deserve, and to level-up every part of the country …honouring the sacrifices made by health and care staff by putting the welfare of the workforce at the top of the agenda. This will require action locally, regionally and nationally. There are financial implications to some of the actions set out. Given the wider economic context, it would be naïve not to recognise the very difficult choices and trade-off in public spending that lie ahead. However, if the government wishes to live up to its promises on promoting health and care, a post- COVID-19 funding settlement will be needed, bringing investment in the health and care workforce, and in social care and public health, where years of austerity have been exacerbated by the pandemic.

These measures are necessary to make good on the promise to 'level-up' society, but they will also need to sit within a wider economic strategy that supports investment in the socio-economic determinants of health. Making progress will also require political courage, not least to push forward, potentially contentious long-term social care reform, given its significant majority. The government is well placed to do this, and should not duck difficult policy decisions".
Source: The King's Fund. Article: "The Road to Renewal: Five Priorities for Health and Social Care", 8 April 2021. Authors: Anna Charles and Leo Ewbank.

Education

Schools in England were closed due to a national 'lock-down' on 20 March 2020 for an unspecified period. However, schools were permitted to remain open to look after the children of key workers and vulnerable children. The Coronavirus Act 2020 came into legal force on 25 March. This legislation gave ministers the powers to close educational institutions and childcare premises. The government also announced that GCSE and A-level examinations would be cancelled for 2020. Grades were to be awarded based on predicted grades and teacher assessments. All primary schools in England began to re-open on 1 June. It was planned that primary-age pupils would be back in school by the end of June. However, on 9 June, the government announced that all primary schools would not re-open. This was due to concerns about the impact this could have on the infection rate. Consequently, most primary school children did not return to classes until early September 2020.

Secondary school in England re-opened for year

groups 10 (ages 14-15) and 11 (ages 15-16) from 15 June. However, schools were instructed to continue to educate young people in those age groups at home and keep face-to-face lessons to a minimum. Secondary schools returned in full at the start of the new academic year in September 2020.

During December (and in light of growing concerns on increasing COVID-19 infections), re-opened schools were instructed by the government to switch to remote home learning until at least the February half-term in 2021. All primary schools in England re-opened on 8 March 2021, whilst secondary schools opened in stages, with flexible timetables.

School Examinations

On 20 March 2020, the government announced that all secondary school examinations were cancelled that year. As a result, an alternative method had to be designed and implemented at very short notice. In their place, qualification grades were to be based on teacher predicted grades, combined with a 'moderation process' to be defined by Ofqual, the education standards body.

A public outcry ensued when, after the release of the A-Level results on 13 August 2020, it became apparent that the moderation algorithms used had delivered some highly controversial results. Following increased pressure and public disquiet, the regulator decided to withdraw the 'computerised' results and regrade students based solely on the original teacher predictions. Before the GCSE grades were published on 20 August, it was decided that they too would be based entirely on teacher predictions.

When schools in England closed to face-to-face teaching in January 2021, the government once again cancelled GCSEs and A-Level examinations due to take place in the summer of 2021. Similarly to the previous year, grades in England would be awarded based on teacher estimates. Teachers would be free in deciding how to assess their students.

It is assumed that many will use questions provided by examination boards, but this is not guaranteed. Alternatively, they could give their mark based on pupils' previous work submitted during their course. Schools and colleges would submit their grades to examination boards by 18 June 2021. The A-Level results will be published on 10 August and GCSE on 12 August.

However, experts warned that this year's approach could lead to significant grade inflation and would be of less value to colleges, universities and prospective employers.

University Education

For the 2020/21 academic year, most English universities adopted a blended learning approach, consisting of a mixture of online and in-person teaching. A Department of Education survey from September 2020 indicated that 39% of students were involved in classroom-based courses that may be adapted to online delivery. 22% of subjects required in-person teaching, and 39% of courses had 'external' contact hours or practical elements. On 25 September 2020, Manchester Metropolitan University locked down two of its halls of residence, placing 1,700 students in isolation for 14 days after some 127 students tested positive for COVID-19.

Home Teaching

Students were encouraged to continue studying at home, with many parents being responsible for their children's education (a debatable legal point). Many teachers continued to set work for and interact with their pupils online. BBC's 'Bitesize' programmes provided a range of resources to help children, young people and adults. Some studies have suggested that many students had completed little or no academic work during the 'lockdowns'. In

November 2020, SAGE, the government advisory group, recorded evidence that pre-school and primary children were less susceptible to contracting COVID-19 than adults. It was unclear whether secondary pupils were less susceptible.

The number of coronavirus infections increased rapidly in the general English population throughout September and October 2020. From early August through to the middle of November, the COVID-19 Infection Survey showed that rates were highest among teenagers and young adults.

In early September, SAGE had warned that large numbers of students presented a 'critical risks' of seeding COVID outbreaks across the UK and said that universities were highly likely to experience significant outbreaks. The potential for the rapid spread of COVID-19 among university students was in residential settings. Consequently, most COVID transmission could be traced back to students living together. Patterns often showed one positive case followed by further cases within the same university accommodation block. However, research found minimal evidence of transmission happening in face-to-face learning environments. The majority of transmission of positive COVID-19 was through domestic or social interactions, being 87% and 76%, respectively.

Source: 'Coronavirus and the Impact of Students in Higher Education in England': Office for National Statistics, 21 December, 2020.

During the pandemic, the most effective tool for maintaining pupil retention and learning access has been 'Digital Classroom' or online learning. However, school closures in response to the pandemic have revealed numerous issues affecting children's access to education. Access issues were particularly experienced by deprived schools, where more than a third of students did not have access to electronic devices or internet access. This lack of access gave rise to public appeals and an initiative launched by the

Daily Mail in England entitled 'Laptop Appeal'. This campaign played a pivotal role in ensuring that children had access to laptops, raising a large amount and encouraging companies and individuals to donate excess laptops. Social mobility and class differences meant that some of the poorest and most disadvantaged children were affected by a lack of access to remote learning.

You're Giving The Gift Of Online Schooling For All
"It's just two days since we asked for your help in providing laptops to pupils whose educational chances are being crushed because they can't access on-line lessons. Your response has exceeded our wildest expectations. In that short time, you, our phenomenally generous readers, have given an astonishing £250,000. As used laptops can be wiped and reconditioned for as little as £15 each, this means that a huge number of young people deprived of on-line teaching during lock-down, will soon be able to benefit form it. As our poll today shows, the situation is desperate, with a massive digital divide between children of affluent households, and those less well off. In countless appeals down the years, as Mail readers, you have shown your willingness to lend a hand to those in need. In the last two days, you have proved that generosity shines as brightly as ever, for a cause that could not be more vital."
Source: Daily Mail, 25 January 2021, page 16.

Social distancing was a massive blow to the education sector. A study by the Office for National Statistics (ONS) carried out in 2019 found that over 60,000 children from 11 to 18 did not have internet access. Pupil rotation and staggering learning meant that break-times were essential for keeping the number of students together in a small space to a minimum. Class sizes have been altered to reflect this need.

OFSTED Inspections

Ofsted inspectors carried out nearly 2,000 visits to education and social care providers during the autumn term of 2020. The reports found that in just over half of the schools visited, pupils in 'bubbles' were sent home to self-isolate at some point during the term. Inspectors heard that repeated absences due to COVID-19 outbreaks resulted in pupils losing more learning. Many children are believed to be at least six months behind where they should be. For a significant number of pupils, repeated periods of self-isolation have gradually chipped away at the progress they have been able to make since September 2020. More pupils were sent home in 'bubbles' in secondary schools than in primaries. Inspectors also found that schools had to provide 'meaningful' remote education under two different circumstances; 'bubble isolation' and 'individual' isolation.

Many schools visited were making real progress with remote provision for 'bubbles', often including live or pre-recorded online lessons. However, pupils who were self-isolating individually, for two weeks at a time, often had a poorer experience. 'Whole bubbles' can more easily be kept up to speed with the planned curriculum where they work at home. However, isolated individuals often miss out on the new content taught to peers' in class'. Instead, they had to revise at home. For those children, the loss of learning they experienced in the summer is repeated.

Commenting on 'remote education', the Chief Inspector of Ofsted said, "While remote education is better than nothing, it is no substitute for the classroom. Schools are struggling to assess whether remote learning is effective or not. For many, the measure of success is whether or not children are engaging with the work at all, rather than whether they are developing their knowledge and understanding; a case of 'remote attitude' rather than 'remote learning'".

Amanda Spielman: HM Chief Inspector-Ofsted, 15 December 2020.
Source: "COVID-19: Isolation having detrimental impact on children's educa-

tion and welfare, particularly the most vulnerable". Third Report: Office for Standards in Education, Gov UK.

At the end of December 2020, the public was demanding answers to questions in respect of children's education during the COVID-19 pandemic:

1. Does going to school raise the infection rates among children? According to SAGE, there was no direct evidence that virus spread within schools played a 'significant' role in increasing infection rates among children. However, there was no evidence that schools do not affect infection rates. If a new coronavirus strain were more contagious in children, the risk could be increased.

2. What happened last term from September to December? Hospital admissions began to rise before schools re-opened in England in the autumn. However, SAGE suggested that classrooms were not a contributory factor in this increase. Evidence suggested no 'consistent pattern' between schools re-opening and the rise in coronavirus cases. However, in Denmark and the Netherlands, cases accelerated after schools re-opened.

3. Would closing schools save lives? Experts suggested that closing schools for a month for those in Tier Four areas could mean fewer hospital admission in England.

4. Would closing schools reduce the 'R' rate? Experts suggest that keeping schools and universities closed would reduce the R rate by around 25%. The latest R rate in December ranged from 1.1 to 1.3. Closing schools for a month could bring it below 1.

5. What will happen when schools do re-open? Researchers believe there can be a 'bigger rebound' if schools were to re-open in February, as the peak in cases would be delayed. Experts have also warned that we need to vaccinate 2 million people a week to

avoid the infections seen in the first wave in March/ April 2020.
Source: Daily Mail, Questions, 30 December 2020, page 6.

Ministers faced a wave of criticism over plans for GCSE and A-Level grades, which would lead to an onslaught of appeals. It is also believed that universities could become over-subscribed by large numbers of students awarded 'inflated' grades by teachers. Under government plans, teachers could determine the grades their pupils received and how they were worked out (whether they used coursework, classroom performance, or use 'mini-exams', based on questions from previous exam papers). Ministers believe this is the only way to assess pupils forced to learn at home, following the closure of all schools at the start of the year.

Critics fear there will be huge inconsistencies in how pupils are assessed. Consequently, 'grade inflation' will make it virtually impossible for universities or employers to assess a pupil's 'actual' capabilities. Grades awarded should be 'meaningful to employers' so not to impede pupils' 'life-chances'.
Source: Daily Mail, 26 February 2021. Page 6. Authors: Josh White and Martin Beckford.

Commentary

"Since the 1870s, when Britain stopped sending children up chimneys, this country has upheld its commitment to the care of the young. As of Monday, when it was announced that all schools Universities could be swamped with too many students this autumn due to teachers' inflated grades. The Office for Students (Of S) urged admissions tutors not to 'over-react' in a year likely to see unusually high numbers of top performers. It stressed that universities will face penalties, including fines for flooding their courses at the expense of 'quality of provision'. This year, A-Level exams will be scrapped for the second time because of the pandemic, with students getting a teacher-assessed grade. Experts have predicted that it will lead to a repeat of last year, when a record 38.1% of grades were A or above, compared with the usual 25%. This inevitably means that a much larger number of students will be eligible for a place at the top universities. The Of S urged institutions to be 'sensible' and avoid 'abusing students' trust' by sacrificing quality for inflated intakes. Chief Executive, Nicola Dandridge said: "It is vital that students starting this autumn do not face further disappointment because the quality of their course is reduced by over-recruitment and poor organisation. Universities and colleges need to plan wisely to ensure that all students have a high-quality experience. The Office for Students will also use its powers to step in where this is not the case".

Universities tend to recruit as many students as they can to generate tuition fee income. Last year, amid the glut of students caused by grade inflation, universities gave out places to a record number of students. The Office for Students revealed that it is investigating some universities already over concerns they may be dishing out mass 'conditional/unconditional' offers. These guarantee a student a place, providing they list the university as their 'firm' choice, but these have now been banned. Critics say they amount to 'pressure selling', and are a ploy to get more students enrolled. The Of S stated: "With the rise in applicant numbers and plans for teacher-assessed grades, universities and colleges are likely to have many well-qualified students to choose from. We expect universities and colleges to do their part to admit and support the most disadvantaged students". In some cases, this will mean looking beyond grades to identify potential by understanding the context in which those grades have been achieved. Many universities already make lower-than-usual offers to students who have faced adversity. The pandemic has hit many of the most disadvantaged groups the hardest. A student from a low-income family without adequate space and resources to study, will likely have faced greater barriers to learning at home, compared to their more advantaged peers. These barriers need to be recognised in the admissions process and beyond.would have to close until mid-February at the earliest, that principle is now in question. It is clear to me, and to other parents like me, that our children are fast becoming third-class citizens. Their education, their rights, future and well-being, not to mention their mental health, during this pandemic have been treated as if secondary to everyone else's. That's not just my opinion. It is a fact, borne out by the actions of teaching unions whose principal aim is not the welfare of children, but the desire to make political capital out of the pandemic, and by a Labour Party with the same selfish, short-sighted agenda, as well as a government burdened with impossible choices. At every stage, it seems, children have been an afterthought. The priority has been protecting the elderly and the vulnerable from the worst effects of the disease, and it is right that those who suffer most should be the ones to whom we afford the greatest protection.

But not at the complete expense of others, and particularly not at the expense of an entire generation so vital to the future prospects and morale of this nation. And yet the message we are sending to our young people is loud and clear: your lives don't matter. As the mother of two teenagers, one doing A-levels this year and the other GCSEs, this notion fills me with a mixture of rage and heartbreak. I am by no means one of those rainbow-unicorn snowflake parents, but God I feel sorry for the blighters. They can't go to school, use a library, see their friends, participate in sport or any extra-curricular activity. They can't even get a job because, thanks to lock-down there are none. The one thing that was keeping them going was getting through the exams this year and the excitement of moving to sixth form or university. Now those prospects have been taken away from them. The exams have been cancelled, and there will be some form of teacher assessment instead.

The decision to sacrifice them may 'follow the science', but it is beyond me. Psychologically, it's hugely damaging. Strange as it may seem, exams are what have been keeping them motivated, the knowledge that they were to be tested and would have the opportunity to prove themselves. Indeed, for those who have struggled with online learning, as so may have, and whose predicted grades have fallen as a result, the chance of making up lost ground in the exams was a glimmer of hope. Take that away, and what's the point in getting out of bed in the mornings? As the daughter of one friend said to me: 'It's like no one cares any more'. Well, I do, as does my mother, who rang me from her home in Italy in a state of anguish. Again, she's no sentimentalist, but on this occasion, and most uncharacteristically, because she is the most level-headed of women, she is spitting tacks. The idea that children, and her own grandchildren, should not matter appals her. The view that schooling is not a front line issue, just as vital as access to healthcare or food, is incomprehensible. From her point of view, teachers are key workers, and schools are just as important as hospitals, and she's right. My kids are incredibly lucky. They are safe, warm and well fed, with their own rooms, laptops, decent wi-fi and food in the fridge. They find their parents deeply irritating, but we are not violent or otherwise abusive. Sadly, that is not the case for every child in this country. And for them, an education is not just useful, but a lifeline. School gives them a refuge from the troubles at home, it offers them an escape from the bad hand that fate has dealt them. The adults they meet at school are often the only ones they can trust. Education gives them a chance to escape the statistical odds stacked against them, to invent their future according to their own hopes and dreams.

The point is that you cannot just put children's dreams on hold. No one gets a second childhood. No one gets to be 15 or 17 again; once it's gone, it's gone. That's why it's not enough for unions and politicians simply to shrug their shoulders and say they have no choice. Yes, we must contain the spread of the virus. But we cannot do so at the cost of young lives. And we must have a proper plan in place to repair the damage being done to the younger generation who, through no fault of their own, are facing an increasingly grim future. If the issue is safeguarding teachers, as so many claim, that's fine. Let's put them at the front of the queue for vaccinations. Many of them are young, so not at serious threat of the virus. But for those over the age of 50, the worry is understandable. Surely it is not beyond the ken of government to vaccinate all those who need it, as we are doing with NHS front line workers. There are about half a million teachers in the UK, it would take just a few days to vaccinate the most vulnerable and, if necessary, family members. I am convinced older people such as my mother would be prepared to shield for a few more weeks, even months, if it meant their grandchildren could go back into the classrooms. And if a child or young person happens to live with a vulnerable adult, prioritise them for vaccination, too. It's not as though we don't have the wherewithal to identify those at risk. You can't buy a coffee these days without it being registered somewhere. Let's use that data wisely and strategically. And if we need to bring in the army to help staff schools, so be it. If we need to scrap the summer holidays to allow children to catch up, we should do so. The schools would understand. I have spoken to several over the past few months and not one has expressed anything other than dismay at the situation.

Teachers are just as distressed as the rest of us, if not more so, particularly since they are seeing first-hand the effects of school deprivation. Eating disorders, self-harm, alcohol and substance abuse are all on the rise among young people. And the longer they remain trapped at home, the worse it will get. What is missing is a coherent, viable

strategy for dealing with the virus long-term. Even if we have a successful vaccination programme, this thing is going to be with us for a good while yet, possibly for ever. We simply can't keep shutting down schools, or society in general indefinitely. We must strain every sinew and explore every possibility to get schools open, and keep them that way. Yes, we must protect the NHS. Yes, we must save lives. But for God's sake let's find a way of doing it that doesn't forget children, or send the next generation back up that metaphorical chimney."
Source: Daily Mail, 6, January 2021, page 11. "No One Gets a Second Childhood": Author: Sarah Vine – Columnist of the Year.

The Economy

The negative impact of lockdown goes far beyond merely controlling the spread of COVID-19. The effects seep into almost every area of social life in England. The UK's economy has already contracted sharply due to government-imposed restrictions to slow the virus's spread. The only hard data available is claims for universal credit. This implies that people have lost their jobs, the number of claims being between five and seven times their normal rate. The most affected sectors are transport, hotels, restaurants, hospitality, non-food retail and some manufacturing. In March 2020, at least 12-15% of the British workforce and the economy was shut down. The COVID-19 crisis has had a catastrophic impact on the UK economy and labour market. At COVID's peak in April 2020, 31% of jobs were 'furloughed', and by January 2021, unemployment had risen to 5%, the highest since 2016.

Although the crisis has affected the entire economy, impacts have varied across sectors. 'Furlough' statistics for the lock-down in January 2021 indicate that 68% of jobs in accommodation and food, 64% in arts and entertainment, and 52% in retail were 'furloughed', making these the worst impacted sectors. In contrast, other sectors have been less reliant on 'furlough', and some have grown their workforce. Health and public administration created an additional 374,000 jobs in 2020, largely to help manage and oversee the response to the pandemic. Other sectors have grown due to accelerated public demand, such as real estate, online sales, IT services and finance.

Economists differ in how quickly they expect the economy to recover once restrictions are eased. Some expect that consumer spending could underpin strong growth. Others believe that an expected rise in unemployment this year will lead to consumers being more cautious. Other sectors that have been partially affected by lockdowns, such as retail, leisure and hospitality, are expecting a rapid recovery once restrictions ease and consumer demand picks up and is sustained. The average forecast among economists is for GDP growth to be about 4.8% in 2021. The Office for Budget Responsibility has forecast the GDP growth at about 5.5% for this year.

Industrial leaders condemned the curfew placed on pubs and restaurants in September last year. Boris Johnson's warning that the 10 pm closing time could be extended for up to six months created fears of mass closures and job losses. Employers and industry leaders warned that cuts could be just the tip of an iceberg that threatens to sink an entire industry employing 3.2 million people.
Many have questioned the science behind the curbs. Kate Nicholls, Chief Executive of the UK Hospitality Trade Association, said: "It is hard to understand how these measures are the solution to fighting the disease, when government data shows just 5% of infections out of the home are related to hospitality. A switch back to working from home, along with a pause of events reopening, means this is now effectively another lock-down for hospitality in city centres. This would be a huge blow for many businesses, unless the government announces a comprehensive package of support swiftly".

Chairman of the Wetherspoon Group, Tim Martin,

said: "The curfew is utterly stupid. We have done a good job at social distancing in pubs, and there is hardly any infections being passed on in pubs". Christopher Snowdon of the Institute of Economic Affairs think-tank said: "A 10:00 pm closing time for all pubs, bars and other hospitality, seems to have emerged from a 'random policy generator'. Whitbread, which owns Premier Inns Hotels, as well as the Beefeater and Brewers' Fayre chains, has put almost one in five of its staff on notice that they may lose their jobs. Chief Executive Alison Britten said: "We are now having to make some very difficult decisions, and it is with great regret that today we are announcing our intention to enter into a consultation process that could result in up to 6,000 redundancies in the UK, of which it is hoped that a significant proportion can be achieved voluntarily". This news came as Whitbread revealed that like-for-like sales fell by 77.6% in six months to 27 August, 2020. Despite the job cuts, it hopes to keep most of its 900 hotels and 350 restaurants open. However, unions condemned Whitbread for axing jobs after using the Government's 'furlough scheme' to retain workers throughout the lock-down. Unite assistant general secretary Howard Beckett said: "Whitbread readily took tax-payers money, it must now uphold its part of the bargain, and put these plans on hold".
Source: Daily Mail, 23 September 2020, "Fears Stupid Curfew Could Deal Crushing Blow to Jobs". Authors: Sean Poulter and Matt Oliver.

The Bank of England warned that working from home full-time poses a long-term threat to the economy. The COVID-19 pandemic may have triggered the largest shift in working practices in modern times. There are obvious advantages to working from home, and many feel more empowered without the daily commuting, and there is flexibility. However, there is also evidence that this shift in working practices could make staff less productive. The lack of face-to-face interaction with work colleagues can threaten the creativity towards full economic growth. Figures from the Office for National Statistics (ONS) show that almost 25% of workers believe their productivity has been negatively affected by home working, compared with 12% who believe it had improved.

The Bank of England did admit that the transition to more flexible working struck a better balance than being stuck in the office five days a week. However, it also cautioned against full-time home working. It argued that it would ultimately make employees less content, less creative and less productive in the long term. Remote working inhibits our ability to cultivate working relationships. ONS figures show just 60% of adults travelled to work between 14 October and 18, down from 65% the previous week. The Institute of Directors commented: "One of the main ways we learn on the job is through interaction with other colleagues. The rise of remote working clearly raises a big challenge". One leading economist predicted that government lock-downs will cost the UK £1.8 billion per day. Economist Douglas McWilliams, the founder of the Centre for Economic and Business Research, said: "Shutting the country down for at least a month will wipe £1.8 billion off the value of the economy for every day it lasts". He forecasts the gloom to push into next year, meaning the UK's coronavirus recession will likely last until the spring of 2021. As Christmas parties are cancelled and high streets are closed, businesses and consumers are expected to slash their spending. This will have a knock-on effect on the public purse as VAT takings slump.

As more businesses struggle on the brink of collapse, job losses are expected to rise despite the extension of the furlough scheme. This will blow a hole in household finances, and banks will increase the number of loans they have to write off as customers fail to meet repayments. Sir Roco Forte, Chairman of Rocco Forte Hotels, said: "The hospitality industry and the whole entertainment industry is already on its knees and this is the final death blow. You can have furlough and other schemes which reduce the businesses outgoings, but if you have no income you can't survive. The second lock-down is a disaster". The restrictions came as restaurants and pubs were gearing up for the Christmas rush to take back some of their lost income over spring and summer. December is an absolutely critical month for businesses. The number of visitors across all shops is expected to fall by 62% on last year. High streets will be hit harder than other locations, such as shopping centres and retail parks. Most consumers are likely to have completed a vast amount of online shopping in advance and may fear returning to high street shops. Business leaders believe that the second wave of coronavirus cases could slash 5 to 10% off economies in the Western world every month that restrictions last. Losing Christmas-related spending will have a distinct impact since December retail sales are about 50% higher than the monthly average. As unemployment bites, many British households will struggle to make ends meet. Forecasters have predicted that banks will have to write off 2.5% of loans to consumers next year, up from 1.3% in 2020.

Source: Daily Mail, 2 November 2020, Page 8. Author: Lesley White, City Correspondent.

Britain faced the prospect of more than a million extra unemployed, a 'double dip' recession and a record borrowing deficit of £500 billion by the end of 2020. Following the announcement of a second lock-down, business leaders predicted a bleak winter with experts downgrading projections which would be a major blow to the country's fragile recovery. They forecast a steep wave of redundancies once furlough eventually ends, leaving more than 3 million people unemployed. At the same time, they warned that government borrowing could hit a record £500 billion in 2020, as the closure of businesses and an 'economic slump' hit tax receipts. They also predicted a double-dip recession with the economy contracting again in the final quarter of 2020. This was due to the month-long lockdown. A 'recession' is defined as two consecutive quarters of economic contraction. The UK economy shrank by 2.5% in the first quarter of 2020 and 19.8% in the second. However, the economy returned to growth in the third quarter (July to September) as restrictions were eased and businesses re-opened. This raised tentative hopes that the UK could pull itself out of its coronavirus recession.

At the beginning of 2020, before COVID-19 struck, 1.3 million people were unemployed. This number increased by the end of the year to 1.5 million. Economists now expect it to surplus three million by 2021 as more than an additional 1.7 million go out of work due to the pandemic. Hopes of a strong recovery from the coronavirus recession had all but retreated in 2020. This was despite the sharpest slump in output since comparable records began in 1955. Businesses that had just begun to see trade picking up and banking on a busy Christmas period were thrown into chaos. Economists predicted unemployment to hit a peak of 8% in 2021 but more recently predicted it could go above that level resulting in three million people out of work. The unemployment rate in November 2020 was 4.5%, the highest for three years, with companies including British Airways, Rolls Royce and Boots axing thousands of jobs. Professor Len Shackleton, editorial and research fellow at the Institute for Economic Affairs, said: "The new lock-down is hugely disappointing. It will lead to higher unemployment and set the recovery back by many months."

Investment bank Goldman Sachs commented that the economy would shrink by 2.4% in the last three months of 2020, while Citigroup analysts forecast a 4% contraction as they fear more protracted national lock-downs.
Source: Daily Mail, 3 November 2020, Page 8. Author: Lucy White, City Correspondent.

In November 2020, more than 9,500 jobs at some of

the biggest high street names were put in jeopardy as England went into lock-down again on 5 November. John
Lewis cut a further 1,500 jobs, adding to the 1,300 already
axed when it permanently shut eight of its stores in July.
Lloyds Bank declared it would make 1,070 more staff redundant on top of the 865 earlier in the pandemic. Clark's
Shoes put all 4,000 of its store staff on notice as part of its
fight to survive.

These losses were compounded when Marks and
Spencer reported its first loss in its 94 years as a listed company. Marks and Spencer, which had already cut 8,000
stores staff since March 2020, had seen its large stores suffer while many of its smaller food halls were located in
empty railway stations and airports. Sainsbury's was also
expected to deal another blow to the retail sector by announcing 3,000 job cuts. More than one million jobs were
expected to be lost before Christmas (2020), even before
the latest lock-down was announced, taking unemployment
past 2.5 million.

The new lockdown restrictions, which started on 5
November, again put the future of High Street stores in
doubt as they approached their peak Christmas trading. The
John Lewis Partnership, which also owns Waitrose, is trying to save £300 million per year in the wake of the virus to
secure its long-term future.

These latest cuts represent almost a third of its
5,000 head office staff and will help the firm save £50 million a year. It has already closed one of its central London
offices and plans to convert excess space on the upper
floors of its Oxford Street site into offices. In 2019 it made
75 of its 225 senior managers redundant. It hopes the plans
will help stall years of falling profits and allow it to make
£400 million a year by 2025.

Sainsbury's is expected to announce redundancies.
It will axe many roles at Argos, which it bought in 2016,
and cut jobs in its supermarkets on the meat, fish and deli

counters. These cuts come despite supermarkets holding up well in the pandemic. The new lock-down, which required all 'non-essential' retails to close, removed half of the available shopping hours between now and Christmas when many firms make most of their annual profit. COVID would leave up to 18,000 UK High Street shops empty as vacancies rose to the highest level since 2013. Lloyds Bank said it would axe 1,070 jobs and hire 300, on top of the 865 cuts it made in September.

Source: Daily Mail, 5, November, 2020, page 26. Author: Tom Witherow, Business Correspondent.

The UK faces plunging into its first double-dip recession since 1975, with the latest lockdown expected to cost almost £400 million per day in January 2021. Output in the first quarter of the year was £24.5 billion lower than it would have been without the third national lockdown in December 2020. The Centre for Economic and Business Research predicted that if the lockdown were lifted in mid-February, it would have cost the UK economy £390 million every working day. Business closures have resulted in output shrinking by more than 4% in the first three months of 2021. Although it is expected that the economy will pick up later in the year as the roll-out of the COVID vaccines allows shops and restaurants to re-open, growth predictions for 2021 are not expected to be significant. It has been put by forecasting groups to be around 5%. With restrictions in place in most areas of the country in January, the British economy faced a challenge at the start of the year. A very modest contraction was seen in the first three months of 2021, resulting in a 'double-dip recession'.

The coronavirus pandemic dragged the UK into its first recession for 11 years at the start of 2020. The country had a brief respite in the third quarter as the first lockdown was lifted, and the 'Eat Out to Help Out' scheme encouraged the public to spend. However, the economy shrunk again in the final quarter of 2020, when COVID restrictions were again re-imposed.

In December 2020, the Bank of England predicted a 1% decline for the final quarter. However, economists believed that the decline would be nearer 2%. Another constriction in the first quarter of 2021 placed the UK back into recession. Even leading into the third lockdown, the economy was already at around 11% below what it should have been.

Concerns about the UK's poor growth have renewed speculation that the Bank of England could cut interest rates to a minus figure to encourage spending rather than saving. The Bank's base rate is already at a record low of 0.1%.

However, there are some signs of recovery. It is expected that the economy will benefit progressively through 2021 with the roll-out of the vaccination programme. It is anticipated that the level of GDP at the end of 2021 will not be lower due to a successful vaccine roll-out. For the 13th time since March 2020, the Chancellor of the Exchequer intervened to keep businesses and jobs viable and to limit the long-term damage to Britain's economic prospects caused by the coronavirus pandemic. The latest intervention in February this year was relatively small and targeted at those smaller retail and hospitality businesses in danger of collapse as the third national lockdown took effect. The bill of £4.6 billion represents just 0.2% of the nation's total output. It appears insignificant compared to the vast extra spend of almost £280 billion on COVID-19 support measures (to date).

This extra spending, together with lost tax revenues, means that the UK will have borrowed more than £400 million over the financial year 2020/21. The national debt – all the borrowing accumulated over decades – has now soared beyond the £2 trillion barrier. The chancellor's measures will only slow down the pace of the slump. Forecasters have predicted the economy will shrink by 3% in January and 3.5% in the first quarter.

The Office for Budget Responsibility has estimated that the average cost of each of the chancellor's 12 spending packages has amounted to around £22 billion. In addition, the Bank of England has expanded its programme of buying government bonds for cash three times since the first lockdown. It has provided an extra £475 billion to the economy since March 2020. The Bank's policy is designed to support consumption, spending and investment. This additional funding can be itemised:

1. Public Services

As the pandemic has progressed, the government has committed to spending an extra £127.1 billion on public services. This includes direct spending on the NHS, the cost of Test and Trace, the ordering, buying and distribution of vaccines, PPE, and extra support for local authorities and social care.

2. Employment Support

In March 2020, the chancellor introduced the Covid Jobs Support Scheme, better known as 'furlough'. He reviewed the scheme in his Winter Economic Plan in September 2020. The cost of this scheme has been estimated at £73.3 billion. Through the 'furlough scheme', UK's unemployment level stood at 4.9% of the workforce in December 2020, against 8.4% in Europe. From October to December, some 370,000 UK citizens were made redundant.

3. Loans and Guarantees

Operating through high street banks, the government has provided £68.2 billion in loans to small and medium-sized businesses. In addition, the Bank of England has a special loan facility for the biggest public, private and overseas-owned companies trading in the UK.

4. Business Support

The chancellor has added £4.6 billion to the package of measures for businesses and enterprises at the cost of £34.1

billion. This package includes the 'tax break' on business rates scheduled to end in April 2021 and the cut in VAT for hospitality businesses currently closed and administered by local authorities.

5. Welfare Measures

The biggest welfare expense has been the £20 per week temporary increase in Universal Credit worth £1,000 a year to recipients. The chancellor has also raised the sums that low-income renters can claim in housing allowances. The bill for Job Seekers' Allowances has also increased, and the total cost of additional welfare payments is projected at £8.3 billion by the end of the financial year in April 2021. The total additional expenditure now stands at £276.8 billion.

Source: Daily Mail: 6 January 2021, page 12. Author: Lucy White, City Correspondent.

Economic Data

Economy

Government borrowing per day	£973m
Total COVID bill for taxpayer	£407bn
Cost of furlough support for self-employed	£107bn
Government borrowing this year	£355bn
Estimated total borrowed for 2020/26	£929bn
Estimated national debt in 2025-26	£2.8trillion
Debt as a proportion of GDP in 2023-24	£109.7%
Economic contraction in 2020	9.9%
Public spending in 2021	54.5% of GDP
Tax burden in 2025-26	35% of GDP
Expected rise in unemployment	6.5%

Expected rise in unemployment in pandemic	900,000
Estimated extra savings by households during the pandemic	£180bn

Retail

185,447 retail staff lost jobs since the first lockdown. 15,187 stores closed at the rate of around 42 per day. There is a 13.7% shop vacancy rate. 35% of money spent was spent online in January 2021.

Hospitality

£86.4 billion was lost in sales across the hospitality industry, and 660,000 jobs were lost. 340,000 jobs lost in the supply chain. 11,894 licensed businesses permanently closed between December 2019 and February 2021. 2,000 pubs lost. £900 million invested by the sector to get COVID secure.

NHS

There were 4.9 million people on the NHS waiting list, with 304,044 people waiting for more than a year. There were 32 million fewer GP appointments in England in 2020 than in 2019. There were 6.87 million fewer A&E attendances than in 2019. 400,000 fewer people were referred for cancer treatment. 43,000 people were believed to have missed dementia diagnosis. 12,000 fewer heart operations took place in 2020 than in 2019. 67,173 trauma and orthopaedic patients waited more than a year for their operations. One in five adults suffering depression during the summer of 2020. 27,000 more people were in contact with NHS Mental Health Services in December than in the same month in 2019.

Source: Daily Mail: 22 March 2021, page 13.

By the beginning of May 2021, the Bank of England forecasted that the gross domestic product (GDP) would soar by 7.25%. This soaring would represent the strongest growth since 1941, when a frenzy of wartime manufacturing ramped up output. Because of the pace of Britain's vaccination roll-out, the economy will return to its pre-pandemic levels by the end of this year. In addition, almost one million fewer people than previously estimated will lose their jobs. The Bank of England believes that the UK is on course for a V-shaped recovery where a steep fall in activity is followed by a sharp rise. Households are now desperate to get out and spend again, which will drive a speedy rebound for the economy.

Commentary

"Spring has sprung for the UK economy. This year it is set to grow at its fastest pace since the Second World War. It is easy to see why. As COVID infection rates have fallen sharply and the vaccination programme has been rolled out, the health risks facing us have plummeted. This is encouraging people to return with gusto to shops, pubs and restaurants as restrictions are lifted in line with the Government's roadmap. Retail spending is already above pre-COVID levels. Travel, football and restaurants and pub bookings are recovering rapidly towards those levels. This is boosting households' confidence and encouraging them to splash more of the £150 billion in cash they stockpiled during lock-down. Surveys suggest a growing fraction of these savings are now being spent, contributing to the 8 per cent growth in household spending the Bank of England now expects in the second quarter of this year, the second fastest quarterly growth rate ever, only behind the third quarter of last year, which came from a much lower base. Some of these savings are also being used as a deposit for as house.

The UK housing market is currently going gangbusters, with transactions and prices rising at pace in all parts of the country, supported by the extension of the stamp duty exemption in the Budget. This bounce in confidence and spending is not confined to consumers. Businesses, too, are putting their accumulated £100 billion of savings to work, with investment intentions picking up and firms' hiring intentions, as reflected in posted vacancies, rapidly approaching pre-COVID levels. With hiring strong, and with the extension of the Government's furlough scheme to September, it is possible that as many new jobs will be created as are lost this year, leading to little or no further rise in unemployment. In its latest forecasts, the Bank revised down its estimate of peak unemployment from 7.75 per cent to less than 5.5 per cent. It is currently around 5 per cent. A year from now, it is realistic to expect UK growth to be in double digits, activity to be comfortably above pre-COVID levels and unemployment to be falling. Such a tennis ball bounce in the UK economy would put it at the top of the G7 growth league table. It is possible this could be the high-water mark for the UK economy. There are certainly still some large risks, including from the virus and from the debts accumulated during lockdown, that could slow or even derail the country's recovery. But my own view is that it is more likely the UK economy will power through, rather than relapse, in the months ahead, moving swiftly from bounce-back to boom.

Having regained their spending and socialising habit, and with money in their pockets, households and businesses will, I suspect, maintain the momentum in demand. Indeed, as long as health and unemployment risks remain low, they will be encouraged to put even more of their savings to work. This could generate a virtuous circle of higher spending, boosting jobs and incomes in ways which support further spending. The key, policy-wise, will be to ensure this boom does not turn to bust. The most likely cause of such a bust, history tells us, is an unwanted bout of inflation. Inflation inflicts collateral damage on our finances, squeezing the purchasing power of our pay and causing rises in the cost of borrowing. And experience during the 1970s and 1980s demonstrates that, once out of the bottle, the inflation genie is notoriously difficult to get back in. By the end of this year, inflation is likely to be above its 2 per cent target, largely due to temporary effects of higher energy prices.

At that point, the UK economy is likely to be growing rapidly above its potential. This momentum in the economy, if sustained, will put persistent upward pressure on prices, risking a more protracted and damaging period of above-target inflation. This is not a risk that can be left to linger if the inflation genie is not, once again, to escape us. That is why, at last week's meeting of the Bank's Monetary Policy Committee, I voted to begin throttling back the degree of support provided to economy. To be clear, this is not a case of slamming on the brakes, but rather gently taking our foot off the accelerator. Doing so now reduces the risk of a handbrake turn-for borrowing costs and the economy down the road, with all of the disruption this would entail for our job and finances. By the end of this year, close to £1 trillion of extra liquidity will have been provided by the Bank to the UK economy since the global financial crash, almost half of it over the past twelve months. This support has contributed importantly to putting the spring back into the economy's step. But with the economy bouncing back, and with inflation risks on the rise, now is the time to start tightening the tap to avoid the risk of a future inflationary flood".

Source: Commentary by Andy Haldane, Bank of England Chief Economist. Daily Mail, 13 May 2021, page 9.

Chapter Three: The Vaccination Race

In December 2019, the UK became the first country to approve a COVID-19 vaccine for emergency use. Oxford University developed a vaccine in January 2020, even before the World Health Organisation (WHO) had even officially named the coronavirus COVID-19. The university was already working on a prototype vaccine against the coronavirus that causes MERS. They realised that they would be able to adapt the chimpanzee adenovirus vector they were using to confer protection against SARS-CoV2. In June 2020, the UK signed a contract for 100 million doses of the Oxford-Astra-Zeneca vaccine. In addition, a separate deal secured access to 30 million doses of the Pfizer-BioNTech vaccine, which was announced in July 2020. This was increased to 40 million doses in October of 2020.

The UK government's Vaccine Task Force, set up by the Chief Scientific Officer Professor Patrick Vallance, was established to help accelerate the acquisition and distribution of vaccines. Since May 2020, the task force, which consists of experts in science, technology and logistics, has secured orders from seven different vaccine manufacturers. This totals 400 million doses – or enough to vaccinate the UK population three times over.

By the autumn of 2020, clinical trial data indicated that both the Pfizer and Astra-Zeneca vaccines were highly effective at preventing symptomatic diseases. Moderna in the US also reported positive results, prompting the UK government to increase its order from 5 to 17 million doses. On 8 December 2020, in the University Hospital, Coventry, 90-year-old Margaret Keenan became the first person in the world to receive a COVID-19 vaccination as part of the mass vaccination programme. Since then, large buildings around the UK have been converted into temporary vaccination sites alongside hospitals and some GP surgeries.

The schedule of priority groups defining the order in which members of the public should receive the vaccine was devised by the government's Joint Committee on Vaccination and Immunisation. This comprised scientists, doctors and other experts. In line with WHO guidelines, the first up were care home residents and health workers, followed by older and clinically vulnerable people. There are, understandably, measurable disparities in the delivery of vaccine doses and challenges to be met while comprehensibly vaccinating every community. Some black and ethnic minority groups were more hesitant about receiving the vaccination. In part, concerns related to whether the ingredients in the vaccines were compatible with religious or cultural beliefs.

Even if the government's aim of full vaccination by mid-February as its target is met, there will still be millions of people waiting in line for their first dose in the coming months. In particular, there is the constant threat of 'new variants' that could evade immunity, potentially requiring the production and roll-out of a new generation of COVID-19 vaccines and 'boosters'. Scientists are already working on this, with Oxford University saying that a 'tweaked' version of its existing vaccine could be available by the autumn of 2021. The government's 'Task Force' has also struck a deal with the German company 'CureVac' to develop new vaccines against emerging COVID-19 variants, agreeing to provide 50 million doses, should they prove effective. The British government is already planning for the third round of booster doses in the autumn. There is also the need for alternative delivery methods to injection, such as nasal sprays or patches, to allow vaccination in pharmacies or even self-administration at home. This could greatly reduce the pressure on hospitals, vaccination centres and health centres. As we learn to live with the virus and its variants, COVID-19 vaccination might become an annual event like flu injections. There is much uncertainty ahead, but the progress of the mass vaccination programme to date is encouraging.

The Oxford-AstraZeneca Vaccine

On 26 October 2020, it was reported that medical and high-risk patients were likely to receive Oxford's COVID-19 vaccine before the end of the year. Leading the project, Professor Adam Hill said that emergency approval of the vaccine would allow those most in need to receive the vaccine while the final trials were still continuing. Full authorisation would allow the rest of the UK's population to receive the vaccine from early 2021. Professor Hill, founder and director of the University of Oxford's Jenner Institute, did admit that the timing was very tight to start vaccinations before Christmas 2020 but that it was not impossible. Two phases of successful clinical trials established that the Oxford vaccine was 'safe' and triggered a strong immune response. The third phase was at an advanced stage. The Jenner Institute was running trials at nine locations in Britain, involving 10,000 volunteers, and other trials were being carried out in Brazil and South Africa. Corroborative partners were also running additional trials in both India and the US.

The 'critical' stage in the development process is the 'unbinding' of trial results. This reveals data from participants given the vaccine compared with those in the 'placebo' group. Until this is completed, neither the participants nor the researchers leading the trials will know who has received the vaccine or the 'placebo'. This process is known as 'double-blinding'.

Researchers plan to seek emergency approval for the most vulnerable patients based on 'interim' results while still conducting more trials to provide firmer evidence. The initial licence would be for emergency use, not

full approval. Professor Hill explained: "The Regulators will want to see more data on safety and efficacy before they grant a licence to vaccinate everybody. What we are looking for this year (2020) is an 'emergency use' authorisation that will allow us to go and vaccinate those most a risk as a priority. Medics and other key workers would also be able to receive the vaccine under an 'interim' licence". Professor Hill suggested that data based on as few as 20 cases of COVID could produce statistically significant evidence that the vaccine is effective. He also suggested that the Oxford vaccine administered with two doses four weeks apart was likely to provide strong protection from COVID-19 because it leads to both antibodies and T-cell immunity. The latter means the body's white blood cells are primed to destroy any tissue that does get infected.
Source: Daily Mail, 26 October 2020: "Oxford Vaccine Ready By Xmas". Author: David Rose.

Research has suggested that coronavirus sufferers can become re-infected within months. Immunity to COVID-19 is short-lasting, resulting in a risk of catching it year on year. This raises obvious questions about the effectiveness of potential vaccines. Results from the world's largest home testing programme questioned the hope that 'herd immunity' can be developed. Any vaccination may be required every six months to remain effective. This would be more often than the annual 'flu' vaccination. The REACT study carried out by Imperial College, London, involved more than 365,000 volunteers across Britain. It found that the prevalence of antibodies in those who had tested positive for COVID-19 had fallen by a quarter from 6% to 4.4% between June and September 2020. This decline suggested that the body's immune response to the virus was short-lasting, as with other coronaviruses like the common cold. However, experts have pointed out that any reinfections would be milder and less dangerous.

Finger-prick blood tests were carried out on the volunteers between late June and September. They revealed that 17,500 had antibodies present, suggesting exposure to the coronavirus by approximately 5% of the total volunteers. Of particular importance, researchers found a decline in antibody levels across all age groups and all regions of England. These findings reveal that levels remained highest in the 18 to 24-year old group and lowest in the over 65s. Significantly, although the number testing positive for antibodies declined gradually in the population overall, levels did remain high among health workers. This suggested that staff in hospitals, care homes and other care settings faced ongoing transmission and repeated exposure to the virus.

It was widely reported in the media during November 2020 that anti-vaccination campaigns were negatively impacting public opinion. To counter this, the government made efforts to enlist celebrities and social media to help promote the coronavirus vaccine amid rising concerns over the spread of conspiracy theories online. There were fears that the 'anti-vax' content on social media sites could lead to a low take-up of the vaccine – affecting the chances of achieving 'herd immunity'.

In November 2020, both the US and the UK found that public willingness to take a COVID vaccine fell by 6.4% after reading 'anti-vax' posts. Under government plans, well-known TV doctors were enlisted, as well as figures with a large following on social media. Religious and community leaders were also consulted to allay possible fears over the vaccine among black, Asian and ethnic minorities.

The Oxford-Astra-Zeneca vaccine was approved for use in the UK from 30 December 2020. The Medicines and Healthcare Products Regulations Agency (MHRA) authorised two full doses of the Oxford vaccine, with the second dose given 4-12 weeks after the first. By the end of January 2021, everyone over 65 should have been vaccinated, alongside younger people in high-risk groups.

Experts advised that giving as many people as possible their first vaccine injection should be the priority before offering previously vaccinated people a second dose. It was highly preferred that a 12-week gap between injections may work better. Unpublished trial results showed that a second injection was up to 80% effective when administered three months after the first dose.

Since the Oxford vaccine was approved for emergency use ahead of a 'full licence' being granted, new details have emerged. Previous data showed that the Oxford vaccine was 62% effective when given as two standard doses. When a half-dose was administered, followed by a full dose, it was increased to 90% effective. A new figure for efficacy was given at 73% when adults received their second dose of the vaccine between four and 12 weeks after the first.

The 12-week gap was seized upon as a way to vaccinate more people with the first dose, while experts stressed that two doses were 'critical for the best and longer-lasting protection'. The second dose of the Pfizer vaccine would be delivered between three and 12 weeks after the first.

Distribution of Vaccines

1. Residents in a care homes and carers (1.5 million)
2. All over-80s (3.3 million) and front-line NHS and social care workers (1.5 million)
3. All over-75s (2.2 million)
4. All over-70s (3.3 million)
5. All over- 65s (3.4 million)
6. Everyone aged 16-64 with underlying health conditions
7. All over-60s (3.7 million)
8. All over-55s (4.3 million)
9. All over-50s (4.7 million)

Source: Daily Mail, 5 January 2021, page 9.

English Vaccinations by Region at 19 January 2021

Number of Doses by Region

	1st Dose	2nd Dose	Total
North West	480,227	60,918	541,145
North East & Yorkshire	610,681	70,633	681,317
Midlands	681,042	65,445	746,487
East of England	370,989	53,146	424,135
South-West	409,060	52,732	461,792
London	367,209	50,016	417,225
South-East	578,287	74,063	653502
TOTAL:	3, 497,498	426,953	3,924,451

Source: Daily Mail, 19 January 2021, page 6.

In March 2021, the NHS wrote to GPs, hospitals and councils to warn of a fall in the supply of vaccines. It drew attention to the Vaccines Task Force warning of a significant reduction in supplies for the week beginning 29 March, which would continue for four weeks. It blamed a reduction in national inbound vaccine supplies and claimed the volume of first doses would be significantly constrained. However, the vaccine manufacturer, Astra-Zeneca insisted the UK supply chain was not being disrupted. Nonetheless, adults would no longer be able to book an appointment at a vaccination centre from 29 March until 30 April. Anyone already booked in for their first or second dose would not be affected.

The NHS insisted that they would continue to ensure that as many as possible in priority groups (including all over 50s and the clinically vulnerable) received their doses. Those in priority groups one to nine could still book for dates prior to 29 March. However, people in lower priority groups (including the over 40s who were next in line) faced a longer wait than expected.

Despite this setback, the government was confident that it would be able to offer the first dose to everyone in the top nine priority groups by 15 April. It still expected to be able to offer the first dose to all adults by the end of July 2021, as previously promised. Everyone would be able to obtain their second dose within 12 weeks of the first.

Regarding the over-40s who were next in line, it was anticipated they would be offered an appointment when a significant number of over-50s had been vaccinated. The over-50s became eligible in the middle of March, and the pace of the roll-out suggested that the NHS would move onto the next cohort by the end of March or early April. This was delayed until May, but some over-40s could be invited for their vaccine after 15 April if supplies allowed. Medics were instructed to focus on maximising vaccine uptake in groups one to nine and offering second doses rather than expanding the vaccine to others. Whitehall sources suggested Astra-Zeneca had informed officials that the firm would not be able to deliver as many doses of the Oxford University-developed vaccine as it had planned. This was owing to a production issue in one of its factories abroad. The UK, Netherlands and Germany were among the countries making the Oxford vaccine. The NHS would still receive enough supplies to offer people a second dose of the Astra-Zeneca vaccine when it was due, and they would also receive supplies from Pfizer. A third vaccine from Moderna was expected to arrive in time from the beginning of April. Brussels threatened to block exports of coronavirus vaccines from the EU and complained about a shortage of Astra-Zeneca supplies. The European Commission Chief said she wanted "reciprocity and proportionality in exports" while pointing out that 10 million vaccine doses had gone from the EU to the UK. Although the Pfizer vaccines were crossing the Channel to the UK, Astra-Zeneca vaccines were not heading the other way. She warned the 'bloc' would "reflect on whether exports to countries who have higher vaccination rates than the EU are still proportionate".

The British government insisted that the two issues were not connected. The UK was not volunteering any of its supplies to the EU, and none of its orders were being siphoned off by Astra-Zeneca.

The Department of Health and Social Care stated that 25,273,226 in the UK had received their first dose of either the Astra-Zeneca or Pfizer vaccines between 8 December and 16 March 2021. Around 1.7 million had also received their second dose. Half of the adult population of the UK is about 26.3 million. Some 95% of people aged 65 and over had received their first dose, as had nine in ten of those clinically vulnerable.

On 17 March, Brussels issued a threat to seize factories and block exports unless Britain gave the EU more COVID-19 vaccines. These threats came even though more than a dozen European centres had halted their roll-out of the Oxford-Astra-Zeneca vaccine over fears of blood clots. The row with the EU came just before it emerged that Britain itself faced a significant reduction of its vaccine supply. The EU Commission President stated that the EU could use powers under the seldom-invoked Article 722 of its treaty. They could potentially be used to seize factories, suspend intellectual property rights for vaccines makers such as Astra-Zeneca, or block more exports of Pfizer vaccines heading for Britain.

Source: Daily Mail, 22, March, 2021, page 6. Author: Jason Groves, Political Editor.

More than a third of older black people had not received a coronavirus vaccination by the end of March 2021. The Office for National Statistics (ONS) found that around four in ten of black, African ethnicity over 70 years of age, and almost three in ten identifying as black Caribbean in the same age group, had either not been offered or had declined vaccination. In addition, one in four older people from Pakistani or Bangladeshi backgrounds had not been vaccinated, compared with fewer than one in ten identified as White British. The ONS report said that older black Africans were five times less likely to accept vaccination than their Pakistani or Bangladeshi counterparts. Based on GP and population records, these figures also break down by religion of older people vaccinated in England between 8 December 2020 and 11 March 2021. They showed that 93% of Christians, 91% with no religion had been vaccinated, compared with 80% of Muslims. The report also found disabled people had a lower rate of vaccination – 87% compared with those not disabled at 91%.

COVID deaths among the over-70s dropped by 97% in ten weeks, thanks to the vaccine roll-out. Towards the end of March 2021, there were, on average, just 32 daily deaths in the over 70s. At the pandemic's peak in mid-January, deaths among this age group had topped 1,000 per day in England. In the second week of January, there averaged 698 daily COVID-19 deaths among the over 80s and 266 among people in their 70s. Nine in ten pensioners and 54% of the entire population of England now had antibodies to fight the virus.

Analysis of death rates indicated that they had fallen most rapidly among groups that had been vaccinated. Less than half of all deaths were now in the over-80s, compared with two-thirds before the roll-out of the vaccines. Data covering the week up to 19 March 2021 showed that deaths fell by 44% among those in their 50s. This compared with a 28% drop among those under 50, most of whom were still waiting for their vaccination. Nearly 55% of adults in England at the end of March had antibodies against COVID, a major study revealed. This increased from one in three two weeks previously and one in five at the beginning of February. The Office for National Statistics (ONS) remarked that 54.7% of people in England tested positive for antibodies in the week up to 14 March. They also found that almost nine in ten over-65s now had antibodies. These figures demonstrate the vaccine's success and indicate widespread immunity among the most vulnerable. The ONS survey also found that 88% of over-65s who had all been offered the vaccine tested 'positive' for antibodies. The rate was 48% among people in their 50s and 41% for those aged 35 to 49. Even among younger people in their 20s and 30s, who had mainly not been vaccinated, more than 40% tested positive for antibodies.

By the beginning of April 2021, approximately 93% of over-50s were vaccinated, with around 31.1 million adults having had their first doses and 4.5 million getting their second doses. The government said that all adults would have been offered their first doses by the end of July 2021. NHS England data covering the period up to 28 March showed that two in five over 80s had received both doses of the vaccine. 87% of people in their 50s had received their first doses, along with more than 95% of those in their 60s and 70s. The astonishing pace of Britain's roll-out means that it had vaccinated a greater proportion of its population than any other major country apart from Israel. The rate of vaccination in England was four times higher than in the EU, where just 11% had received a vaccine at the beginning of April 2021. Oxford University was currently carrying out a clinical trial on children to test the safety and efficacy of its vaccine in younger age groups, with initial results expected in the summer.

No coronavirus deaths were reported across England during the second week of May – for the first time since the pandemic's start. It marked an end to a bleak 14 months in which fatalities had been announced every day, with 127,609 Britons losing their lives after testing positive. At the peak of the crisis on 20 January, the daily toll reached 1,820. On 10 May, there were just four deaths across the UK. This significant milestone confirms the success of the vaccination roll-out, with two-thirds of all adults having now been vaccinated. The majority of people in every age band over the age of 40 had now received the first vaccine. However, a substantial proportion of those who do catch COVID, some also with underlying health problems, were still unvaccinated. There was also a risk of significant spread in the younger age groups. A third of adults have received both doses of the vaccine, including all of the most vulnerable and elderly. Daily cases by early May among the over 70s in England had fallen to just 54. At the peak of the crisis in January, there were more than 6,000 cases per day in this age group.

Recorded cases during January stood at 68,053. Hospitalisations were at their lowest level since July 2020, with fewer than 1,000 COVID-19 patients in wards in England. It was confirmed in early May that just one dose of the Astra-Zeneca or Pfizer vaccines cut the chances of dying by 80%. Two doses of the Pfizer vaccine slashed the odds of dying by 97%, according to Public Health England's (PHE) latest figures based on the effect of those given the vaccines. A separate report found further evidence that the Pfizer vaccine was highly effective at reducing the risk of hospital admissions, particularly for older patients. The vaccine programme estimated that at least 10,000 lives had been saved, with one in three adults fully vaccinated against COVID. Analysis of almost 50,000 people who tested COVID-positive between December 2020 and April 2021 concluded that vaccines offered 80% protection against death.

It was announced by the government's vaccines

minister, Nadhim Zahawi, that "Britain will treat COVID like the 'flu' with an annual vaccination programme". He believed that the UK could keep coronavirus under control through regular booster vaccinations starting as early as autumn this year or early next year. They would be given at the same time as the 'flu' vaccine, with one in each arm. Government advisers were still undecided on whether a third dose should be given, which vaccine to use, and who would get one. They considered offering a booster shot to all adults or a shot limited to groups such as the over-50s or the most vulnerable, including care home residents.

Vaccines may also be adapted to target new variants if necessary. Early trial results suggest it may be safe to mix jabs, so those who have had the Oxford-Astra-Zeneca may be able to get Pfizer or vice-versa.

Capacity at Public Health England's Porton Down laboratory was expanded, enabling scientists to more rapidly test vaccines against new variants as they arise.

COVID-19 New Variants

There are thousands of different variants of the coronavirus circulating across the world. Viruses mutate all the time, and most changes are inconsequential. However, others make the disease more infectious or threatening, and these mutations tend to become dominant. Those variants with the most probable concerning changes are called Variants of Concern or VOCs. There are kept under the closest surveillance by health officials. These include the 'Kent' or Alpha variant (B.1.1.7), prevalent in England, where more than 200,000 cases have been identified. The 'Brazil' or Gamma variant (P.1) has spread to more than ten other countries, including the UK. The 'South Africa' or Beta variant (B.1-351) has also been identified in the UK. Finally, the 'Indian' or Delta variant (B.1.617.2), of which more than 75,000 cases have been identified across the UK. There is no evidence that any of them causes much more serious illness for most people. As with the original 'Wuhan' virus, the risk remains high for people who are elderly or have significant underlying health conditions.

However, a virus being more dangerous and infectious will lead to more deaths in an unvaccinated population. All these variants have changed their 'Spike Protein' - the part that attaches to human cells. The latest Delta variant has some important 'Spike Proteins' such as L452R, making it spread much more easily. However, there is no evidence to indicate it causes more severe disease or might make current vaccines less effective. High numbers of cases of infection increase the risk of mutations. The more a virus spreads, the more chance it has to mutate. Thousands of small changes have been seen in coronavirus, but most with little impact.

Some mutations do lead to 'new variants'. Every so often, a virus changes in a way that helps it survive and reproduce. These variants can then become the 'dominant' type. The genetic code for each of these variants is highly different. The 'Kent' or Alpha variant is of Type B.1.1.7 with the N5 014 mutation. The 'Brazil' or Gamma variant is of P.1 Type with two mutations, N501Y and E484K. The 'South African' or Beta variant is Type B.1.351, with the same two mutations as the Gamma variant. Finally, the present UK 'Indian' or Delta variant is of Type B.1.617.s with two mutations, P681R and L 452R. The N501Y mutation seen in the Kent, South African and Brazil variants may help the virus to spread more easily. The E484K mutation seen in the South African, Brazilian, and other UK variants may affect the antibody response to infection. The P681R and L452R mutations may help the present Delta variant spread more rapidly.

More variations of the coronavirus will continue to emerge, but vaccines can be tweaked to match them. Whilst current vaccines were designed for the earlier versions of coronavirus, scientists believe they should work, although possibly less well. Laboratory research suggests antibodies can fight COVID-19 infection, triggered by vaccination against the Delta variant. However, experts are confident that existing vaccines can be redesigned to tackle emerging mutations.

The UK government has a deal with biopharmaceutical company CureVac to develop vaccines against future variants which can bind to cells more easily and are more infectious. The E 484K mutation is extremely worrying because it may help the virus evade antibodies, allowing re-infections and making vaccines less effective. This variant was first seen in the UK before Christmas 2020, prompting a travel ban on South Africa. Around 105 cases have been found in the UK. Until the beginning of February 2021, they could all be linked to international travel. However, 11 have been detected in people who had not recently travelled abroad. This suggested that the virus spread within the community because infected people without symptoms had flown into the UK. These 11 cases without links to international travel were located in eight different parts of the country. These ranged from London to the West Midlands and Merseyside.

Most of these had no contact, which suggests 'pockets of spread' in several locations across England. The actual number of cases in the UK is likely to be considerably higher because the 11 cases were only identified due to the UK's genomic sequencing programme, which tests a random sample of between 5 and 10% of all positive COVID-19 cases. However, there is a 'high probability' that some of the remaining 95% of positive cases were also the Beta strain. To date, there is no evidence that this variant is more deadly or makes people more ill. However, it is more transmissible than the original 'Wuhan' strain and spreads at a similar rate to the Kent or Alpha variant, which is up to 70% more infectious. Of most concern is the high rate of mutations, which may help it 'escape' antibodies. In January, researchers from South Africa found it contained mutations that may be resistant to immunity from earlier COVID infections.

Health officials have played down concerns that the South African variant could jeopardise the UK's vaccination programme. Initial evidence shows existing vaccines are slightly less effective against it but still offer good protection. Tests were ongoing to see if the Pfizer and Oxford vaccines (the two used in the UK) were effective. Public Health England (PHE) was in a race to break any chain of transmission to rid the UK of the South African variant effectively. It launched 'Surge Testing' in affected areas. All adults in eight postcodes, around 80,000, were to be offered tests whether or not they had symptoms. Mobile testing units were deployed, and officials went door-to-door urging people to be tested. Positive samples underwent genomic sequencing to identify which variant they were. However, some experts declared 'surge testing' as futile. While door-to-door testing was a highly visible way to encourage people to stay indoors, it could come at a cost. During a pandemic, it seems unwise to employ people to go from one home to the next, potentially spreading the very diseases they are trying to constrain.

We may never know whether the South African variant originated in South Africa. One similar to it had certainly been detected in the UK, but it is possible that the same random mutation occurred 'independently' in Britain.

Britain leads the world in genomic-sequencing of the virus. We identify these new variants because we are better at looking for them. That is why we detected the Alpha or Kent variant. This initially provoked such panic in Europe that some ports were closed to British traffic for a time. We became the 'pariahs' of Europe, penalised because we are so good at monitoring mutations in our highly effective fight against the virus. Not only are we among the best at genome sequencing, but we are also way ahead when it comes to the number of people we are vaccinating. Most vaccinations will inevitably lead to new variants, as some versions of COVID evolve to 'survive' vaccination.

However, there is no reason to panic. We can identify new variants so simply and adjust the vaccines accordingly. The latest vaccines are being engineered to counteract new variants as and when they emerge. In this respect, we are winning the race.

The Indian-Delta Variant

Experts believe the strain B.1.617.2 could be more transmissible than the Alpha variant. These new variants of the coronavirus pose potentially lethal dangers. With the appearance of the Delta variant in May, ministers did not rule out introducing local lock-downs in those areas where the Delta variant was increasingly prevalent. These included Bolton in Greater Manchester, Blackburn with Darwen in Lancashire and parts of London. Analysis of swabs taken by the UK's biggest variant trackers found 55% of positive cases in Bolton. Nearby, Blackburn had the second-highest infection rate in England, with 90 cases per 100,000 people in just seven days. In addition, almost 54% of samples from Bedford and 77% in South Northampton-shire were confirmed as the Delta variant.

Public Health England (PHE) confirmed that UK cases of the Delta variant had trebled in the course of one week from 520 to 1,700. Fuelled by one of the country's highest infection rates, Bolton saw 437 cases in a week, bringing the average to 152 per 100,000 people. This increase in Delta cases has been driven by people travelling back and forth from the sub-continent. While more than 90% of the residents of Bolton over 65 years of age have had their first dose of the vaccine, public health chiefs in Bolton were concerned that 'take-up' in the worst affected neighbourhoods was 10% below the national average. In May, the Royal Bolton Hospital had only one COVID ward, but health chiefs feared the surge in cases would see admissions rise from the single figures. It was reported that scientists were concerned that fully vaccinated people had become infected with COVID-19 in India itself.

The Delta variant was upgraded by Public Health England (PHE) from a 'variant under investigation' or VUI to a 'variant of concern' or VOC. Initial cases in April and early May were linked to overseas travel, but the increasing numbers of infections pointed to widespread community transmission. It was unknown exactly how these infections were spreading, although there was a suggestion that cases had increased through work or religious gatherings. It was only travellers rather than whole households who were required to quarantine, so family members could unknowingly be spreading the virus.

The 'Delta' variant B.1.617 has three genetically similar subtypes. These are B.1.617.1, B.1.617.2 and B.1. 617.3. This variant has 13 mutations that separate it from the original Chinese COVID-19 virus. However, the P681R and L.452R mutations are of most concern. Scientists believe that these two mutations have the potential for the virus to transmit faster and to bypass immune cells made in response to 'older' variants. In 2021, the second Delta Variant subtype (B.1.617.2) was upgraded to a 'virus of concern' (VOC) because of its spread in the UK. While it is hoped that the vaccination programme can offer good protection to many, the more cases there are, the more severe the disease and the more hospitalisations and deaths would occur, particularly in those unable to be vaccinated or where the vaccines have not worked.

At the time of writing, Public Health England (PHE) had stated that there was insufficient evidence to indicate that the Delta variant caused a more severe disease. Other experts suggest that the high mortality that has been seen in India is more likely to be the result of both increased infection levels and its healthcare system being overwhelmed.

Scientists are testing whether the Delta variant is capable of 'immune escape'. Immune escape happens when antibodies created following vaccination or prior to infection may not prevent a person from becoming infected. There is some laboratory evidence that suggests the Delta mutations are 'escape mutations' and that they could make vaccines less effective. However, scientists also say that reinfections are more likely to be milder than primary infections. Also, continuing research has shown that the vaccines in present use continue to provide good levels of protection against all existing variants.

BioNTech, the manufacturer of the Pfizer vaccine, have confirmed that the vaccine will not require 'tweaking' to protect against the current variants. In addition, an updated vaccine by Moderna successfully neutralised both the South African and Brazilian variants in laboratory tests.

It has been claimed that existing COVID vaccines

will overcome the new Delta variant. Analysis conducted at Oxford University does suggest that current vaccinations were preventing serious illness and death from the new variant. It was of particular significance to note that those hospitalised by this variant, in such 'hotspots' as Bolton and Blackburn, were primarily people who were eligible for the vaccine but had not taken it. The seven-day average for Delta cases in Bolton by age group per 100,000 population were as follows.

60 years and above	9
Between 40 and 59 years	30
Between 0 and 39 years	52

The government stated that only those in eligible categories 'nationally' could be vaccinated in the Bolton area. Consequently, this would have ruled out most adults under 38. Despite this ruling, local health officials in Bolton were using such factors as deprivation and living in multi-generation households to justify young people being eligible for the vaccine.

In mid-May, the infection rate in Bolton was around ten times that of the UK average, being 294.2 cases per 100,000 residents. Mark Logan, Bolton North East's MP, stated that "Bolton must be fast-tracked for vaccination. We must get the first dose out to all over 18s by the end of the month (May) as a priority". All adults in Bolton were urged to book a vaccination. The town was the worst affected in Britain, with infection rates at 12 times the national average.

Despite calls from government ministers not to invite healthy people under 36, Bolton's health officials began vaccinating teenagers as young as 17. Over the weekend of 22nd and 23rd May, 6,000 people were vaccinated. Similarly, in neighbouring Blackburn-with-Darwen (with the third-highest infection rate in the country), an extra 1,000 daily vaccinations were given. In order to circumvent national guidelines, residents were told that even going shopping for a grandparent constituted being an unpaid 'carer' and made them eligible to receive the vaccine.

This massive effort to boost 'herd immunity' comes among rising case rates, particularly among the under-30s in these areas. Low vaccine take-up could have been driving the Delta variant's rapid spread. With 400 cases recorded on 19 May, London had the highest levels of the variant, accounting for almost a third of cases in England. However, only around 25% of these cases involved people who had travelled back from India. This would suggest widespread 'community transmission'.

Experts were particularly worried that the Delta variant was up to 50% more transmissible than the UK Alpha variant. Consequently, it will become dominant in England. While ministers were confident that the existing COVID vaccinations would be effective, they warned that millions had yet to be vaccinated. Such unvaccinated people could prompt a 'third wave' of the pandemic, resulting in more hospitalisations.

Ten Worst Areas For Vaccination Uptake

Region	% of Over-40s
London East	82.0
North	82.0
North-West	82.2
South-East	85.9
South-West	87.4
South East	88.3
North West, Cheshire & Merseyside	88.4
North West & Greater Manchester	88.5
South West	88.5
East England	88.5

Source: Public Health England (May 2021).

By the second week of May 2021, the Delta variant had spread rapidly, with a 79% rise in the number of places in which it had been detected over just one week. Random tests revealed that it was found in 127 out of 314 local areas across England, compared to 71 the previous week, an increase of 40%.

Outbreaks of the variant, which experts now believe could be 50% more transmissible than the Alpha strain, were prominent in the North-West of England and London during May. Data from the Wellcome Sanger Institute highlighted the spread at which this variant spreads, with 23 areas reporting the 'dominant' strain. However, most of these areas had fewer than five recorded cases, and over 40 health authorities recorded just one positive sample.

The Delta variant accounted for eight in ten cases in Bolton, Blackburn, Sefton on Merseyside and Bedford. On 19 May 2021, Bolton still had the most average weekly infections at 210, while Blackburn was second with 76. It was announced that 'Booster-Shots' were to be tested in a world-first trial. Almost 3,000 people aged 30 and over were recruited for a third vaccination ahead of a likely roll-out in autumn.

Such is the state of the UK's surging vaccine programme at the time of writing. Scientists want to observe peoples' immune response to the Delta variant and that of the Alpha and Beta variants. This immune response will be measured following the third dose of Pfizer, Oxford-Astra-Zeneca and Moderna vaccines or new ones on order for Britain. They will also track the side effects of a 'booster jab', asking volunteers to keep electronic diaries for seven days following the 'booster'.

This study which was expected to produce preliminary results by late August or September, was intended to assist officials in determining which vaccines were used if a winter 'booster' programme were to go ahead. They would then have to decide if only a specific age group, such as older people, should receive a top-up vaccine. It would also supplement evidence from vaccine trials of how quickly peoples' immunity to coronavirus waned so that they required a follow-up injection to boost their protection.

Volunteers would be recruited at 18 sites across the UK, including Southampton, Oxford, London and Liverpool, to receive a 'third' vaccine dose ten to twelve weeks after their second dose. Some volunteers would be given half-doses to analyse whether less vaccine is needed. The study, backed by £193 million of government funding, would look at people of working age, aged 30 or over, and a separate group of those aged 75 and over, to see how they respond to 'booster' shots.

Half would have previously received the vaccine from Oxford-Astra-Zeneca and half the Pfizer vaccine. Some would receive the same again, whereas others would get the Moderna vaccine currently rolled out in the UK or Johnson and Johnson's 'Jenssen' single-shot. This shot would be in time for the potential autumn 'booster' campaign to protect people over winter.

According to a recent study, the Delta COVID variant had not caused a national rise in infections. Researchers from the Zoe COVID Study have said there was no clear evidence that this variant was any worse than the Alpha or Kent variant. They believe it was highly unlikely to overwhelm the NHS or stop the UK from emerging from lockdowns. It was also likely that outbreaks would remain predominantly localised.

Swab taken in tests at five-day intervals revealed that new daily symptomatic cases of the variant in the UK remained unchanged at around 2,750. What did emerge from this study was that infection rates varied widely between regions in England.

The lowest number was in the South-East at one in 5,403, the highest in Yorkshire and Humberside at one in 728. On 21 May, the 'R' rate in the UK was 1.1, but only 0.8 in the South-East. Infection rates were spreading more rapidly in the North-West and East of England, where the

'R' rate was 1.3. From 6,000 swab tests taken 2-15 May, scientists identified 'localised clusters' of outbreaks and suggested the virus remained 'under control nationwide'.

This study previously identified local outbreaks of the South African and Brazilian variants, which did not take hold across the country. The number of daily new cases reported during May was around 2,750, which was fairly low and unchanged. This did demonstrate that the Delta variant had not altered the numbers significantly. The only well-observed pattern was localised hotspots. One positive aspect of the Delta variant was that it was not generally translating into increased cases of hospitalisation and fatalities.

Research by Public Health England (PHE) suggested that vaccinations have saved over 13,200 lives and kept 40,000 people out of the hospital in England. Based on figures from Bolton (one of the variant 'hotspots'), nine in ten patients hospitalised with COVID-19 had not received both doses of the vaccine. By the end of May 2021, more than 38 million UK adults had received their first vaccine dose, including 24 million who have had both doses.

Recent research by King's College, London, shows that just one in four people in the UK experienced mild 'side-effects' after receiving the vaccine. Of particular concern was that the average age of those testing positive at the time of writing (July 2021) was 29, a further sign of the success of the vaccine roll-out in older people. Two-thirds of hospital cases were under 25 years of age. However, patients admitted to hospital with COVID-19 were now younger but got less sick and went home sooner. This was further evidence that vaccinations broke the chain between infection and hospitalisation. The number of people ending up in hospital was consistently lower than in previous waves. Even in virus 'hotspots', there was a decline in patient numbers.

Significantly, NHS Trust leaders reported 'three

consistent features' regarding hospital admissions at present (July 2021):

1. COVID-19 admissions were consistently lower than in previous waves.
2. Patients admitted were, on average, younger and with less requirement for critical care. They required treatment in general rather than acute beds and had lower mortality rates.
3. There were very low numbers of COVID-19 admissions where patients had two doses of the vaccine, and protection had built-up past the second dose.

Most of those patients hospitalised after both vaccine doses had other significant health conditions. Confidence has grown that vaccines have broken the chain between COVID-19 infection and high levels of hospitalisation and mortality.

The Delta variant makes up most of all UK cases at the time of writing. Data shows that those who have received both vaccine doses make up less than 5% of those now hospitalised with the variant.

However, regarding the vaccination programme, it will now take until October to vaccinate all the under 30s according to the current rates. Demand for vaccination among young adults has plummeted by 80%, causing the roll-out to slump to its lowest to date. Only 18,000 under-25s a day have come forward for their first dose in the week commencing 18 July 2021. This is a dramatic fall since the vaccine programme was launched to all adults in April. In the week prior to 18 July, more than 90,000 under-25s received the vaccine every day. Up to 22 July, these have now declined to just 31,000 a day during the week ending 24 July.

At this point, the UK's vaccine roll-out is crawling along at its slowest level since it began eight months ago. Back in March, more than 500,000 people were getting vaccinated every day, with first doses peaking at 752,000 in one day. Some experts believe the fall in demand shows Britain is getting close to the limit uptake, among rising concerns over vaccine hesitancy in the young, with three million under 30s still unvaccinated. Low immunity levels in young adults mean that the virus is rampant in those age groups, raising fears that the epidemic could spiral out of control in the UK. Officials commented that many young people do not see vaccination as a priority, with uptake slower on "sunny days, and days when England played in the Euro 2020".

The latest data from the Office for National Statistics (ONS) shows that just 67% of people aged 16-24 currently have no antibodies to COVID-19. In comparison, 92% of all adults in England tested positive for antibodies produced by the body following either vaccination or injection. This rises to 97% among people in their 50s, almost all of whom have now received both vaccine doses. Officials launched a major drive to get younger adults to come forward to help Britain reach 'herd immunity' before autumn 2021. On 19 July, Boris Johnson announced that vaccine passports would be made compulsory in nightclubs and other crowded venues in England from September 2021. The latest NHS figures showed that 33% of those aged 25 to 29, and 36% of those aged 18 to 24, had not yet had their first dose, compared with 88% for all adults. Data up to 8 July showed that the population of the UK having had at least one dose of vaccine was 45,697,875. This represented 68.6% of the population. Those fully vaccinated with both doses was 34,374,246, representing 51% of the population. The following two articles reinforce the vital importance of vaccination in the fight to control the coronavirus pandemic. Both contributors are respected experts in their medical and scientific fields of study.

"What Every Young Person Who Fears Jab Must Be Told" Analysis

"The backlash against COVID vaccines among young people is the most dangerous medical misunderstanding of our times. Fuelled by bogus information on social media, it is not only putting hundreds of thousands of young lives at risk, but threatening the entire country's recovery from the pandemic. The latest NHS figures show that nearly a quarter of Britons aged 30 to 34 have not yet had their first dose. That rises to a third of people aged 25 to 29 and even more, 38 per cent of 18 to 24 year olds. Yet, this week, *The Mail* revealed that these age groups are no longer coming forward for their jabs. Demand for the vaccine among young adults has plummeted by 80 per cent.

Just 18,100 under-25s a day were given their first dose in the past week, compared to more than 90,000 in the week to June 18. Clearly, there is still a terrifying level of vaccine hesitancy among the young, even though the arguments for vaccination are overwhelming. Having the jab is also in the younger age groups' interest. Without collective immunity, many of the good things in life, holidays abroad, gap years, music festivals and sports events, might never properly return. The most common objections of young people to vaccination ca be described below.

[1] Young Only Get Mild Symptoms

It is entirely false to assume that because a bout of COVID seems mild or asymptomatic, it cannot leave lasting damage. Young people, especially the under-30s, are very unlikely to die from the infection itself, but they are by no means exempt from what follows. Figures show around one in ten people aged 18-49 go on to develop long-term symptoms after having the virus, regardless of how unwell they were initially. Furthermore, around one in nine people aged 17-24 and one in six aged 25-34, still report symptoms 12 weeks after testing positive.

'Long COVID', the lingering after-effects of the infection, can be life-changing. As a hospital consultant, I am now seeing many patients whose health has been dramatically affected by the prolonged symptoms that often follow a mild case of COVID. Around a million people in Britain are now believed to have 'Long COVID'. It's exhausting, debilitating and often very frightening. As yet, there's no cure. This is a virus like no other and we're still learning about the havoc it can wreak on the lungs, the heart and other major organs. People who refuse the vaccine because they imagine COVID can't hurt them, are literally gambling with the rest of their lives.

[2] I Had COVID So I Don't Need The Jab

We don't know how long antibodies and immunity last after a COVID infection. What we do know is that there are numerous cases of people catching the virus for a second or even a third time. And many people wrongly assume they have had COVID because they have had the symptoms (the persistent cough, the high temperature, and the loss of senses of taste and smell), but without a positive antibody test, no one can say for certain that they've caught and overcome the virus. A vaccine is a highly effective insurance policy against the disease, one which research has proven lasts at least six months.

[3] The Tests Were Too Rushed

This is a regular source of concern and anxiety. But consider the difference between the programme and all others. Never before have so many scientists worked together, combining knowledge and pooling their results, in a global effort with a single goal. The result was a set of vaccines that have proved highly effective against a brand new virus, and the UK jabbing programme was conducted with military efficiency. It's the most ambitious, daring, brilliant human accomplishment in decades. Why wouldn't every single person, whatever their age, want to be part of that? The speed at which it has all been done is part of the marvel. Trials that would normally take many years have been accomplished in weeks, because such vast resources have been made available. But no corners were cut. All the various vaccines – Astra-Zeneca, Pfizer, Moderna and the rest, had to undergo rigorous safety checks. The vaccines have been tested on tens of thousands of people before being made available.

In Phase One and Phase Two clinical trials, jabs were tested on small numbers of volunteers to check they were safe, and to determine the right dose. In Phase Three trials, they were tested on thousands of people to see how effective they were. The group who received the vaccine and a control group who received a placebo, were closely monitored for any adverse reactions or side-effects. And safety monitoring continues to this day.

[4] Trials Didn't Test For Side-Effects

Sheer nonsense. The whole point of vaccine trials is to weed out the drugs that have unexpected side-effects. In Australia, the government withdrew an order for 51 million doses of a vaccine being developed with the University of Queensland, because it was shown to trigger false positives in HIV tests. The country's health secretary, Bredon Murphy, pointed out that the vaccine was probably effective at blocking serious COVID infection, but it had this unwanted repercussion that could make it difficult for doctors to identify new cases of HIV. Rather than take that risk, the whole programme was scrapped. That's just one example. More COVID programmes have been abandoned than have succeeded. The trials were exceptionally rigorous.

[5] I'm Worried About the Risks

One of the main concerns the young raise is the risk of blood clots from the Oxford-Astra-Zeneca jab. But in

May, the Joint Committee on Vaccination and Immunisation announced the under-40s wouldn't be offered Astra-Zeneca due to the extremely small risk of blood clots. The risk of side-effects from the vaccines they were being offered is very low, although they commonly include a sore arm or feeling achy or sick. The point is almost all drugs potentially have a side-effect. Packets of paracetamol, for instance, list skin rashes, itching, swelling of the mouth or face, shortness of breath, mouth ulcers, bleeding gums, unexplained bleeding and more. But people still take them because, as with the vaccine, the likelihood of any of these happening is so very small. When we hear of people becoming ill or even dying after a vaccine jab, it's easy to jump to conclusions about side-effects. It's much harder to take a rational view and accept that coincidence plays strange tricks.

Part of my work as an oncologist involves developing and trialling potential cancer vaccines. A few years ago, I was due to give a patient an injection of an experimental new drug in the hope that it would prevent complications in the progress of his disease. The vaccine was manufactured in America and sent by air.

When it arrived at Heathrow, customs officials refused to release it immediately. I went to bed that night cursing the red tape. Next morning, my patient was dead. He had suffered a catastrophic bleed on the brain, which was both tragic and unexpected. If I had administered the vaccine as scheduled, his death would have meant the complete cancellation of the trial. No doctor would ever have dared take the risk again. We would all have assumed that the drug, in some way that could not be discovered, had fatal side-effects. Every time I read of blood clots or other inexplicable 'side-effects' of the COVID vaccines, I remember my patient. If his death reminds us how coincidences can seem to skew scientific data, it will not be in vain.

[6] Vaccine Will Change Our DNA

One consequence of the pandemic is half the country think it's no longer necessary to spend seven years at medical school to become an expert. People use the jargon of epidemiology and genetics as easily as they used to discus last night's new Tik-Tok sensation.

Much of the information that is shared on social media is about as scientific as a *Godzilla* movie. Lizards do not grow into man-eating monsters when exposed to radiation, and vaccines do not change our DNA. The misunderstanding might arise because some vaccines use modified mRNA, to stimulate the immune system by triggering it to produce proteins which are similar to those on the surface of the coronavirus. This is revolutionary science, but it does not affect the body's basic DNA.

[7] Big Pharma Can't Be Trusted

Of all the anti-vaxxers' arguments, this is the only one that makes sense. As a general rule, the pharmaceutical giants can't be trusted completely because whenever they launch a new drug, they have tens of millions of dollars at stake, and this means that there is often a temptation to draw conclusions that favour the commercial interests of their products.

But in the case of the COVID vaccines, everything is different. To encourage companies to work fearlessly in developing a drug to save the world, the government has guaranteed they will not be penalised for mistakes as long as there is complete honesty and transparency. In other words, the drugs companies stand to lose everything if they attempt any cover-ups. They could face fines running into many millions of pounds. But as long as they hold nothing back, we can trust them with our lives.

[8] It Might Make Me Infertile

The fear of infertility has made many young women reluctant to have the vaccine. But there is no reliable evidence, none at all of which I am aware, that proves the jab has ever affected fertility. The unknown effects of 'Long COVID' are likely to be much more serious. This virus can have really dreadful effects on internal organs. Please don't take the risk. If you are planning to get pregnant, get inoculated.

[9] It Could Damage Immune System

This is another fundamental misunderstanding of how the virus works. COVID poses the most dangerous threat to people with compromised immune systems. That typically means the over-55s (the age at which natural immunity begins to decline), and in the over 75s (who might sometimes have no effective immunity left at all). But many younger people have compromised immune systems too. There's often no way of knowing, until it's too late. You really don't want to find out by suffering a serious bout of COVID. In the wake of reports that people who have been doubly vaccinated are still catching COVID, some are arguing that this means the vaccine is ineffective. Actually, the reality is quite the opposite. Those getting ill will have severely depleted immune systems. The only thing saving them, quite probably, is the vaccine. Without the jabs, they might have died. And there are no proven cases of new allergies being triggered by a COVID vaccine."

Source: Professor Angus Dalgleish, Vaccine Expert: Daily Mail. 23 July 2021, pages 8 and 9.

"We Have To Keep Calm and Carry On Jabbing" Commentary

"Keep calm and carry on vaccinating, that is the best advice for ministers and the public alike as another COVID panic appears to be taking hold. Today the country takes a giant step towards normality, with the reopening of restaurants, pubs, cinemas and much else. But we also face news that the so-called Indian variant of COVID (actually three new variants) is starting to spread rapidly in the UK. It is prompting some scientists and politicians to call for a pause in unlocking and a delay to 'Freedom Day' on June 21 when potentially all legal limits on social contact are removed.

One of the new variants (all of which originated in south Asia) appears to be up to 50 per cent more transmissible than the Kent variant that emerged about six months ago and which prompted another national lock-down. It sounds frightening, but there really is no reason to panic because we are in a very different place from where we were then. Today, we've got the solution to the pandemic in our hands – the science is working and the vaccines are breaking the train of transmission and deaths.

From the start of this global crisis, we were always banking on vaccination to get us out of it and there's no reason to change our strategy or lose faith in what scientists have delivered. The truth is that we were always braced for more variants. That's how a virus works: it evolves. Epidemiologists knew the coronavirus would mutate as it spread, and that the basic laws of evolution mean the more successful variants oust the old ones.

At the moment, the Indian variant in Britain is confined to a few hotspots such as Bolton and Blackburn with Darwen, but pretty soon it is likely to be the dominant strain of COVID throughout the UK. That's the stark reality of viruses and it shouldn't be used to stoke up 'coronamania'. I strongly suspect the new variant has existed in this country for at least two months. Even before the first calls were made back at the start of April, to put India on the 'red list' and block incoming flights, there will have been cases in this country.

Boris Johnson is being criticised for not banning

visitors from the sub-continent until the last week of April. Political opponents say he was wary of causing offence to the Indian prime minister, Narendra Modi, ahead of trade talks. But the virus knows no borders. If the mutation couldn't arrive directly from India, it would have entered the UK via some zigzag route from other countries not on the red list. Indeed, by the time we identified it as a new variant, it was already too late to keep it out.

The Kent variant was picked up very quickly because Britain leads the world in genomic analysis. It took much longer for a new strain to be identified in India, where DNA testing is not done on anything like the same scale. Yes, the images we have seen from India are alarming and tragic with hospitals overwhelmed, a shortage of oxygen and ventilators, and thousands of funeral pyres. It has prompted some observers to warn of a third COVID wave in the UK, with up to 1,000 deaths a day being forecast by some.

I do not believe this will happen. For one thing, India has a population at least 20 times greater than Britain's and in many cities people live in very close quarters. That means the virus spreads more easily. And the fact that mass gatherings – for sporting events, political rallies and religious festivals – were permitted weeks after the outbreak began has made the problem much worse. Most crucially, the vaccination programme in India lags far behind ours (despite the fact that India manufactures more vaccines than any other country).

We have an 'immune-competent' population, that is, more than two thirds of adults in Britain have now had at least one vaccination, and a third of the unvaccinated cohort – largely younger adults, have immunity from contracting the virus itself.

The vaccine is not an impermeable barrier against COVID. But all the evidence, including the patterns in India, shows that people who have been inoculated will not contract a serious COVID infection or be hospitalised. The best data shows that 90 per cent of people who have had both jabs will be immune to infection. The rest will probably not be ill enough to have a transmissible viral load. That is to say, they won't be able to pass it on. And 90 per cent of people eligible for the vaccine are accepting it. Despite the rampant disinformation and scaremongering on social media, only ten per cent of those eligible are refusing the jab, although of course, I'd like to see that number fall.

The vaccine is not an instant solution. It takes at least a week for immunity to kick in, and there has to be a minimum delay of three weeks between the first and second jabs. We must continue with our much improved test-and-trace programme and to urge anyone who is showing COVID symptoms to self-isolate. In cases where that could mean financial hardship, there should be grant payments to support families, especially in deprived areas. As I write, the emergence of the Indian variant is no reason for us to abandon the road map, plotting our path back to normal life. Vigilance and vaccination are the watchwords."

Source: Daily Mail, 17 May 2021, page 9.
Commentary by Professor Brendan Wren: Professor of Vaccinology at the London School of Hygiene and Tropical Medicine.

Chapter Four: A Statistical Overview of the Pandemic

For the UK, the response to the COVID-19 pandemic was the need to balance actions aimed at reducing deaths from the virus with the negative impact of restraining economic and social activity, including reduced access to health and public services. Understanding the number of confirmed virus cases and deaths resulting from the pandemic is essential.

We can estimate the overall impact of the pandemic by comparing the number of positive cases detected against the number of registered deaths recorded each week since January 2020. Such data can then be compared with the average deaths and confirmed cases, including July 2021, when this work concludes. This is the yardstick by which we can assess the success of measures being taken by the government to contain the pandemic.

By this means, a statistical overview of the progress of COVID-19 can be carefully monitored and appropriate action taken.

This chapter aims to provide the reader with an accurate statistical assessment of the data available from various sources, covering the progress of the coronavirus in the UK from January 2020 to July 2021. This overview also incorporates studies and surveys carried out by several government-commissioned institutions. This is further supplemented by valuable data supplied by the Office for National Statistics, NHS England and Public Health England. These agencies provide government departments with vital data to inform government policy in controlling the pandemic.

Throughout the coronavirus pandemic, the reproduction number 'R' has been employed to measure whether the virus is under control. It indicates how many people, on average, one person with COVID-19 will infect. Keeping the 'R' number under one has been a major aim of the government's response to the pandemic. However, researchers have claimed that a more useful indicator for controlling the virus is a measure referred to as 'K'.

'K' reveals the pattern the virus spreads. Consequently, a 'K' value of one or above would indicate that a virus spreads more 'evenly' throughout a given population. However, a 'K' number under one would indicate the virus spreading in 'clusters' rather than 'evenly'. This is significant because it provides key information about how we can keep the COVID-19 virus under control.

According to research carried out by the London School of Hygiene and Tropical Medicine, it has been estimated that COVID-19 has a 'K' value of between 0.1% and 0.5%. This would suggest that it spreads in 'clusters'. As a result, scientists now believe that between 10 and 20% of people with COVID are responsible for transmitting 80% of infections. These are so-called 'Super Spreaders'.

Most people infected with the virus will not pass it on to anyone. While the 'R' figure shows the average of how many people are infected by one person, the 'K' figure shows the variation in transmission. Research has shown that COVID-19 is a highly over-dispersed pathogen that spreads in 'clusters'. Using 'K' rather than 'R' as a control measure would be a better way of approaching COVID-19.

The government's policy is to attempt to prevent every infection, which is virtually impossible and probably not even required. Most people who do get infected with COVID-19 do not pass it on to others. The crucial task is dealing with those environments which encourage 'cluster spreading' and limit them in terms of exposure. For example, indoor, insufficiently ventilated environments and gatherings can be linked to most infections.

The first case of COVID-19 was reported in the UK

on 28 January 2020, and by the first week of March, confirmed coronavirus cases had increased to 87. However, by the second week of March, a surge in the virus brought cases to 1,543 and the deaths of 55. Then on 9 April, the UK recorded its highest daily deaths at 938.

A survey of 11,000 people living in England conducted on 14 May, suggested that one in 400 people were infected with the virus. By the first week of June, the death toll stood at over 40,000. It was not until early August that there was a substantial decrease in both confirmed cases and deaths. By 10 August, cases had dropped by around 90%, with deaths down by 5,000. At the beginning of August, a study conducted by Imperial College, London, suggested that approximately 3-4 million people in England had COVID-19. This was almost ten times higher than the official government figures had suggested. At beginning of October, the UK reported 22,961 cases in 24 hours, and by the end of that month, one million cases.

However, from around the middle of November 2020, infection rates of COVID stopped increasing across England. Cambridge scientists published a new model which showed that levels had ground to a halt in virtually every region. The 'R' rate had fallen below 1, suggesting that the epidemic was no longer escalating. The growth rate for England was estimated to be at 0.0 per day. This meant that nationally, the number of infections had stopped growing. It should be remembered that during November 2020, England was in a national lockdown. Consequently, this reduction in peoples' movements (due to legal restrictions) had an expected impact on the figures for infection.

Plots on the 'R' figure over time demonstrate a clear 'downward' trend. The lower values of 'R' were very likely to result from the various 'social distancing' interventions imposed. A weekly surveillance report published by Public Health England (PHE) on 19 November 2020 revealed that COVID-19 case rates in England had fallen for most adult age groups. However, the report did indicate that the highest infection rates were among those 20-29-years at 362.1 cases per 100,000 population during the week to 15 November. This was slightly down from 389.9 the previous week.

Infection rates had also dropped among those in the 30 to 60 age groups. There had been slight increases in those aged between 70 and 79, a rise from 146.1 to 147.5. Those aged 80 and over had risen from 235.5 to 257. These PHE report figures for the number of infections were for the seven days until 21 November 2020.

By the end of November, infection rates for COVID-19 began to fall, together with those for mortality. Official figures indicated that Britain had passed the 'peak' of the virus's Second Wave. This was reflected in case rates which fell across every age range and in all regions of England. It was widely expected that this would lead to fewer hospitalisations and deaths.

Public Health England's weekly surveillance reports indicated that infection rates had fallen significantly between the 16 and 22 of November 2020. More importantly, there was also evidence in 2020 that hospital admissions were falling for the first time. These were down to 15.5 per 100,000 population in the week to 22 November, having been 16.8 the previous week.

The weekly Office for National Statistics (ONS) Survey, which randomly tests tens of thousands of people each week, confirmed these reductions in infection rates. It was estimated that in the week ending 22 November, 633,000 people in England had COVID-19: a reduction from 664,700 in the previous week. The survey also reveals that infection rates had fallen among all adults over 35 years, including the elderly.

A further report from the NHS Test and Trace programme found the numbers testing 'positive' for COVID in England had fallen 9% week-on-week. This was the first time there had been any fall in the figures since the summer of 2020.

A complementary set of data produced by a King's College, London research team estimated that the 'R' rate was down to 0.9. This strongly suggested that the epidemic was indeed shrinking. Despite this optimistic outlook and completely unexpectedly, within just one month, there occurred a dramatic increase in the rate of new infections. By the end of December 2020, a record 39,237 positive tests were confirmed. Infections had surged by 61% in one week.

In addition to this, the number of patients in hospital was to overtake the April peak of 2020. Scientific advisers at SAGE had forecast that the 'R' number could be as high as 1.5 in Eastern England and London, with some intensive care units having reached full capacity. In addition, there were 20,917 COVID-19 patients in hospitals across the country. This was now fast approaching the 12 April 'peak' of 21,683.

On 23 December, 2,004 patients were admitted to hospitals, together with 744 deaths being recorded, the highest since 29 April. This unprecedented surge resulted from a new variant first detected in Kent (Alpha). This led to a ferocious exponential growth in cases primarily in London, the South-East and South Wales. This new outbreak showed no signs of slowing down. On 23 December alone, London recorded nearly 10,000 new cases.

Four out of seven NHS regions in England reported having more virus patients than at any point during the first pandemic wave. These four regions were South-West, Midlands, the East and South-East.

Intensive care units (ICUs) at some hospitals, including the Royal London in Whitechapel, had reached their maximum capacity. On 23 December, SAGE issued the latest estimates for the 'R' rate. It put the rate at between 1.1 and 1.3 in the UK, increasing from 1.1. and 1.2

the previous week. It also estimated that in London and the East, it was between 1.2 and 1.5.

This rate meant that every ten people would infect between 12 and 15 further people. The scientific experts believed that the new Alpha variant increased the crucial 'R' number by around 0.5, explaining the significant surge in the number of confirmed cases. Unless schools remained closed at the time, it would be virtually impossible to keep the 'R' figure below one – until more people had been vaccinated.

Across England, more people were testing positive for the new variant than for the 'original' coronavirus. In London alone, it was found that around 2% of people had the new variant compared to 0.8% of those testing positive for the original virus. This new variant was not believed to lead to more severe illness. However, the higher number of infections meant that the 'knock-on effect would be reflected in the number of hospital admissions.

A further survey by the ONS revealed that one in 50 residents in England had the COVID virus between 27 December 2020 and 2 January 2021. This meant, in effect, that more people were being infected than were being vaccinated. On 5 January 2021, an all-time high of 60,916 positive tests were recorded, with 830 deaths. In addition, hospital admissions also hit a high at 3,351 (above the April 2020 'peak' of 3,099).

Official figures revealed that the overall infection rate rose by 70% during the last two weeks of December 2020. London was the country's worst affected area, with an estimated one in 30 infected. Hospitals in the capital had more than 6,800 COVID in-patients.

The ONS finding of one in 50, or one million cases, was up from one in 70 to 115 in early December 2020. For comparison, during the summer of 2020, this figure stood at one in 2,000. The most revealing figures were those of people who had died of COVID-19 in 2020. This was recorded as the highest annual total since the 1918 influenza pandemic. There were 608,002 deaths recorded in England and Wales, and deaths registered in England and Wales in 1918 were 611,861.

However, changes in the age and size of the population meant that this was not a like-for-like comparison. The population in England and Wales in 1918 was approximately 34 million, compared with around 60 million today. Consequently, proportionally more people died in 1918 than in 2020. From a historical perspective, there have been more than 600,000 deaths in only two years since records began in 1838. The first was in 1940, when around 581,537 deaths were recorded. However, because of an increasing population, deaths in England and Wales were higher in the years of the 1970s and 1980s.

Excess deaths in 2020 were estimated at 91,000 across the UK. This meant that mortality had increased to 15% above the five-year average. It was the greatest upward leap of any year since 1940. Considering rising population mortality rates in 2020, this shows that more than one in 10,000 people in England and Wales died during the year. This mortality rate was the highest since 2003 when the death rate was recorded as above one in 10,000.

2020 ended a period of 17 years in which increasingly good health led to people living longer. The number of 'excess deaths' last year was way beyond expected, even considering the coronavirus pandemic's impact.

Significantly, there were lower than average 'flu' deaths during the first three months of 2020. ONS figures show that 31.2% of deaths registered in the final week of December 2020 were of patients with 'symptoms' of COVID-19. There were 3,144 deaths in which coronavirus was noted on death certificates.

This was the greatest number of COVID- linked deaths in one week since May 2020. These ONS figures are based on the numbers of registered deaths and an analysis of the death certificates on which doctors mentioned the 'presence of COVID-19'. These figures differ from the 'daily' Public Health England (PHE) count, which records the deaths of people "within 28 days of a positive test for COVID".

According to PHE, there were 10,069 deaths in England and Wales registered during the week ending 1 January 2021, this being 1,451 fewer than the previous week. Deaths attributed to COVID-19 were the 'highest' proportion of deaths involving the virus since the week ending 1 May 2020. These ONS figures suggest that the virus continued to take the greatest toll among the oldest age groups. There was no noticeable increase among younger people.

However, in the week ending 1 January 2021, the number of deaths involving COVID-19 in England and Wales increased in most age groups compared to the previous week. The only exception was among people in the 45-49 age group. However, more than 75.3% of deaths involving COVID-19 were still in those people aged 75 and over.

For 18 January, the seven-day figures for COVID cases (37,475) suggest a downward trajectory and that the UK may have passed the peak of the 'third wave of the pandemic'. However, on the same day, 599 total COVID-linked deaths indicated an increase of 70 from the previous week.

Despite this, nine in ten local authorities in England, including every borough in London, saw COVID rates fall in just one week. Experts believe that this sudden dip represents the impact of 'lockdown' restrictions rather than the effect of vaccinations, which were unlikely to have been seen until at least February at the earliest. Official figures suggest that hospital admissions started to ease, with 3,569 recorded in England on 16 January. This was down from a peak of 4,134 just five days earlier.

With national restrictions being imposed on 6 January, confirmed cases were halving. NHS England reported that the numbers in hospitals had fallen by 9% over just one week. On 28 January, there were 30,846 patients in English hospitals. These were down from a peak of 34,336 on 18 January. All seven NHS regions in England recorded a week-on-week decrease in daily hospital admissions. However, despite this positive outlook, the country's largest surveillance testing study found that cases were falling at a much slower rate than during the first lockdown.

Testing of 167,642 people between the 6 and 12 of January found a 'suggestion' of decline, but overall infection numbers remained high. The REACT (Real Time Assessment of Community Transmission) Study, led by Imperial College, London, and commissioned by the government, found that 1.57% of the population of England (around one in 64) were infected by COVID-19.

The infection rate was highest in London, particularly among younger age groups. One in 25 Londoners aged between 13 and 24 years had tested positive for the virus. Even though there was this suggestion of a downturn in the virus's progress, it was not as rapid as that seen in the first lockdown. Also, compared with the first lockdown, more people went out to work and school during January 2021. The REACT study estimated the national 'R' rate at 0.98, indicating that the epidemic was 'shrinking' but only slowly.

Going into February, the study reported that infection levels had fallen significantly by more than two-thirds since the January surge. One in 196 people was infected with COVID during the first half of February, the equivalent of 0.51% of the population of England. The 'R' rate was estimated to be at 0.7, indicating that the epidemic was shrinking.

This study found that levels of infection were halving every two weeks. At this rate, the daily number of cases would amount to less than 1,000 by the second week of April. The previous round of data obtained by REACT covering 6 to 22 January estimated the 'R' number at 0.98, with one in 64 people being infected. Researchers on the study found that the 'R' rate was below one in all areas of England except the North-East. Cases fell among all age groups. However, they did remain highest among those aged 5-12 and 18-24 years. According to official figures for February, the number of deaths attributed to COVID-19 halved within three weeks. There were 4,079 COVID deaths in the week to 19 February, a decrease of 1,612 from the previous week.

The decline in deaths since the third wave peak at the end of January was considered 'dramatic', being down from 8,433 in a single week to less than half. In addition, deaths among the over 60s, the vaccinated group, were also halving every week. Non-COVID deaths were also at a very low level, meaning that by the end of March, the overall death rate would be less than average.

According to the ONS figures, doctors connected 29.5% of all deaths to the coronavirus in the week up to 19 February. Across the UK, the number of deaths registered that week was 15,577, this being 2,374 higher than the five-year average. Of these deaths, 4,447 involved COVID-19 (29.5%). Public Health England (PHE) reported on 2 March that 343 people had died within the 28 day period. This brought the UK total to 123,296 deaths. The total laboratory-confirmed COVID cases stood at 4,188,400 in the UK. By 22 March, Coronavirus deaths had fallen to their lowest level in almost six months, when only 17 deaths were registered. This was the lowest figure recorded since 28 September 2020 and showed a decline of 75% in just one week. The overall suggestion was that COVID infections were 'plateauing'. This led experts to express that the figures were further proof of the UK's leading vaccine programme, which had, by this time, delivered the first dose of vaccine to 28 million people.

On a record-breaking weekend (20-21 March), 1,119,314 people received their first dose. During a peak hour on what was dubbed 'Super Saturday' (20 March), 27 people also received a second dose of the vaccine, followed by another 367,006 on the Sunday (21 March). By the third week of March, more than 50% of the UK adult population had received a vaccine, with almost 2.3 million fully vaccinated with a second dose. These positive figures were a relief to officials as the country marked a year since the first national lockdown on 23 March 2020. Some 126,172 deaths have been recorded in the UK up to this date.

The seven-day average of hospital admissions was around 450 patients, close to the same as the end of September 2020. Some 6,162 patients remained in hospital, which was the lowest level since mid-October 2020. Significantly, this was also more than six times lower than the peak of 39,248 in mid-January, when more than 100,000 patients with COVID were admitted to hospitals in January alone. Most regions of England recorded at least one day free from any COVID deaths for the first time in six months, during the week ending 26 March 2021. Five out of nine regions were completely free of deaths for a minimum of 24 hours. London averaged 1.5 deaths each day over a week.

On 24 March, official figures show no virus deaths in the South-East, West Midlands, Yorkshire and Humberside, or the East of England. Deaths elsewhere across the country fell to a five-month low, with a daily average below 80, compared to more than 1,000 for most of January 2021.

Public Health England (PHE) reported that cases of COVID had 'plateaued' down in every age group, except for schoolchildren who saw a 'modest' increase. It was also found that infections during March were highest among those children aged 10 to 19, with around one in 1,000 testing positive for the virus. Many showed no symptoms. The infection rate rose to 63.5 per 100,000 population among the 5-9 year-olds. All other age groups showed a week-on-week reduction.

Following the vaccine roll-out, infections were lowest in those people aged 70 to 79, at 13.3 per 100,000. In mid-January, there were 34,000 severely-ill patients in hospitals, and by mid-March, these had reduced to just 4,000. By the first week of April 2021, one in 1,000 over 65s tested positive for COVID-19 the previous month (March).

The UK's REACT Survey tracking the coronavirus outbreak found that cases plummeted by 60% between February and March, as millions were vaccinated. The figures reveal that vaccination was 'breaking the link' between infections, deaths and hospital admissions.

The Imperial College, London Survey, commissioned by the government, found that one in 500 people in England tested positive in March 2021. This was down from around one in 200 in February and one in 64 at the beginning of January. In addition, around one in 1,000 over 65s tested positive, down from almost one in 1,000 back in January 2021.

The REACT Survey found that infections were lowest among older groups, almost all of whom had been vaccinated. Prevalence of the virus was highest among schoolchildren at about one in 250. The study also noted that the lower rate among older adults was consistent with an effect of the vaccination roll-out in England, which had focussed initially on older people, and the most vulnerable.

Statistical Disparities

"Claims that Britain will almost inevitably be hit by a third wave resulting in tens of thousands more deaths were called into question yesterday. Government scientists warned this week that returning to normality from June 21st could lead to a surge in hospital admissions on a similar scale to January's 'peak'. However, it has emerged that some of the modelling published by SAGE, was based on 'overtly pessimistic assumptions'. For example, some of the projections assumed that the Astra-Zeneca vaccine reduces the risk of death by around 80%, despite real-world data suggesting that the true figure is closer to 100%. Even the most optimistic of the models in which hospitalisations and deaths are minimal, still make the assumption that the vaccine does not completely protect against serious illness from COVID-19.

Professor Tim Spector, an epidemiologist at King's College, London, accused SAGE of "repeatedly making bleak forecasts that never come true". He insisted: "They seem to be picking the most pessimistic of the assumptions each time, in order to come up with the worst-case scenario, perhaps to avoid complacency. I think the vaccine is doing better than they are saying, and they are just painting a much bleaker scenario than reality".

Meanwhile, Dr Rosemary Leonard, a GP in south-west London said that she was: "fed up with the lack of balance in the modelling predictions of COVID". Of SAGE's modelling, she said: "All very negative, with suggestions that vaccines are not very effective. How about some realistic positive predictions, based on current excellent outcomes from our vaccine programme?"
Source: Daily Mail, 7 April 2021, page 4. Author: Eleanor Hayward, Health Correspondent.

Towards the end of April, it was reported that experts regarded COVID cases in the UK as 'close to the bottom' and that a 'third wave was less significant than feared'. Figures showed that every region in England had 'no COVID deaths' during the week ended 30 April and that the epidemic was retreating. In the seven days up to 26 April, only one death was reported to have occurred within 28 days of a positive test across the entire North-East of the country.

With a population of 2.7 million, the North East had six days with no recorded fatalities. The East Midlands had four days with no deaths. London, the South-East, West Midlands, and Yorkshire with Humberside had three days. Official figures show that the number of patients with COVID in hospitals in England had dropped to the lowest level in seven months.

According to NHS England, 1,310 COVID patients were in hospital on 27 April. This was the lowest recorded figure since 1,299 on 21 September 2020 and was down 96% from the record 34,336 on 18 January 2021. The number of deaths caused by COVID-19 in England and Wales had fallen to just 260 per week in mid-April. This meant that about one in 40 deaths in the week ending 23 April had direct links to COVID infections.

Overall, there were fewer than 1,000 virus-linked deaths of all recorded deaths in April. The figures showed that COVID-19 caused 941 deaths in England and Wales. These compared with 4,144 deaths in England from heart disease (23%) and 4,018 attributed to dementia and Alzheimers (23%). From November 2020 until February 2021, COVID-19 remained the most common cause of death in England. COVID remained the third most common killer during March. In total, there were 38,899 deaths in April in England, 6.1% below the five-year April average. This was the first month since August 2020 in which England saw below average deaths.

The mortality rate for the COVID virus was 20.6 per 100,000 population in England. That was about one in 5,000, the lowest level since September 2020. From January to March 2021, the most common pre-existing condition for deaths due to COVID-19 was diabetes, identified in almost a fifth of all COVID-related deaths.

It was during the last week of May that daily cases of COVID-19 began to rise above 4,000 for the first time in almost two months. There were also concerns over the spread of the 'Indian' or Delta variant. The 'R' rate went above one for the first time since mid-January. Government advisers stated that the 'R' figure was between 1 and 1.1. This is evidence that the epidemic was growing again, up from 0.9 and 1 in the space of one week.

While it was expected that case numbers would rise again as the country exited the latest lock-down, figures released on 28 May show that there were 4,182 new cases, with average daily numbers increased by 24% from the previous week.

Patients in hospitals with COVID were younger and less sick than those hospitalised in January. However, cases of the Delta variant were doubling every week. It only takes five or six such 'doublings' to get as many as a quarter of a million cases. Despite this alarming forecast, on 1 June, zero coronavirus deaths were announced across Britain for the first time since the pandemic struck the UK in January 2020. This milestone underlines the extraordinary power and success of the vaccination roll-out. It was the first day since 11 March 2020 when no fatalities from COVID-19 were recorded.

At the beginning of June, deaths averaged six per day, hospital admissions remained stable, and the number of Delta virus patients was falling in the town of Bolton in Greater Manchester, where this variant had been rampant. In total, 127,782 have died since the pandemic's beginning up to June 2021. At its peak, on 20 January 2021, the daily death toll was 1,820. NHS England data for 2 June 2021 reported 776 COVID patients in hospital, down from 1,071 at the beginning of May. In January, when the NHS was overwhelmed, the number of virus patients in hospital had peaked at 39,249. In Bolton, Greater Manchester, COVID-19 in-patients fell to 42, down from 49 the previous week, with no new admissions. Infections fell following the introduction of Surge Vaccinations in the town.

However, cases were still rising in other areas of the

North-West. Blackburn-with-Darwen (in Lancashire) had the highest rate in the country at 416 cases per 100,000 population at 2 June, the national average being just 30. Of particular importance was that the Delta variant was not establishing itself more widely across the country. Another feature was that virtually all recorded cases were among the unvaccinated.

At this point, scientists remained divided about the re-opening and lifting of COVID restrictions planned for 21 June in England. Some scientists were calling for it to be delayed until everyone had been vaccinated. Currently, there are still many people who have neither had the virus nor been vaccinated. The country is in a vulnerable position in the light of this revelation. Dropping 'social distancing' could be a retrograde step, given the potential of the Delta variant.

In early June, the number of deaths involving COVID-19 each week in England and Wales did drop below 100 for the first time in nearly nine months. A total of 95 deaths were registered in the week ending 28 May. In the UK as a whole, just 106 of the 10,977 deaths during the same week mentioned COVID on the death certificate – accounting for just 0.9%.

Although infection rates had increased to 170% since the beginning of May, deaths registered on 9 June were only 13, and hospital admissions remained flat. These figures emphasise that the link between COVID infections and death had been broken for the first time. Dying from influenza is now about ten times more likely than being killed by the coronavirus. Data demonstrates that when the second wave was at its peak in January this year, approximately 45% of deaths registered in England and Wales were linked by doctors to the COVID-19 virus. The last week of May recorded the lowest weekly deaths since the beginning of September 2020.

ONS figures cover the period after the rise in infections due to the Delta variant, which provoked fear of a 'third wave' of the virus. Daily infections rose by about a third in April to just under 3,500. When the 'second wave' hit its peak during the week ending 22 January, 8,422 COVID-19 deaths were registered in one week in England and Wales. In January 2021, 25,716 people died with COVID symptoms in England. This was roughly 20 times the number who died in the same month from influenza and around five times the death rate for dementia or heart disease.

During the week ending 28 May, there were 9,628 deaths registered in England and Wales; 232 fewer than the previous week and 3.1% below the average for the same week in the five years to 2019. According to official figures, COVID-19 caused just one in every 125 deaths in England and Wales in early June. According to ONS data, symptoms of the virus were present in only 0.8% of people who died during the week ending 11 June. Almost 14 times as many deaths were attributed to 'influenza and pneumonia'. The total of 84 COVID-related deaths was the lowest recorded since the beginning of the pandemic in January 2020. This was further evidence that the link between COVID infections and deaths was breaking down.

Across the UK, there were 93 COVID-linked deaths, and this was the first time the number of weekly deaths across the whole country dropped below 100 since the 'second wave' in the summer of 2020. Across the UK, the number of deaths registered in the week ending 11 June was 11,611 (285 more than the five-year average). However, the 93 COVID deaths were 15 fewer than the previous week. Between the pandemic's start in January 2020 and 11 June 2021, death certificates recorded 132,434 COVID-linked deaths in England and 7,897 in Wales. At 1 July 2021, 26,068 new COVID cases were detected, indicating an increase of almost 70%. These were the highest figures recorded since late January.

The daily hospitalisations due to COVID-19 were rising at 263, an increase of 6.4%. However, these were well below the January peak at 4,579 in one day. Daily infections in July were running at around 2,000.

With just over 60% of the UK's adult population now fully vaccinated, the impact of the current Delta variant is significantly reduced, though this variant appears more transmissible than the 'Kent' or Alpha variant of the second wave in 2020. This is further evidence, together with the figures for daily hospital numbers, that vaccinations have broken the link. Hospital numbers remained essentially flat during the current wave of infections. This was in stark contrast to the sharp upward trajectory seen last year. At the same stage of last year's wave, hospital admissions were over 7,000, compared with 1,720 in these latest figures.

Most dramatically, statistical analysis shows how Britain's vaccination drive all but demolished the link between infections and deaths. The seven-day rolling average number of deaths in the UK is currently at about 17. At the same stage of the second wave last year, this figure was 122, more than seven times higher. Current COVID cases are now around 26 times higher in young adults than in the elderly. This is further proof that vaccination protects the most vulnerable in society. Public Health England's weekly forecast on 1 July shows that hospitalisations and deaths remain stable. The recent surge of Delta infections has largely been confined to young adults. On 1 July, 26,068 confirmed cases were recorded in the UK, the highest of any figure since the end of January 2021. Whilst weekly cases have increased by almost 72%, deaths and hospitalisations have only increased by 10% at present.

One disturbing development is that the steepest rise in cases has been among those in their 20s, the last age group to be vaccinated. Experts believe this surge has been partly fuelled by fans gathering to watch England matches at the 'Euro 2020'.

The weekly infection rate is highest among those aged 20 to 29, with 424 cases per 100,000 population. This is 26 times higher than the weekly case rate in the over 80s at 16 per 100,000. Cases have risen in all regions of England and age groups in the first week of July 2021. The North-East has overtaken the North-West as the worst-hit region of England.

Researchers have also identified a surge in cases of the Delta variant in popular holiday resorts in the South-West, including Cornwall. In addition, places such as the East Midlands and London are now seeing higher rates of change. With the summer holidays approaching, there is also an increased risk of infections. According to current research, daily COVID cases are on track to top 100,000 before the 19 July' Freedom Day' as football fans drive a ferocious surge in infections.

The UK's largest study tracing the spread of the COVID virus has found that cases have quadrupled over one month (June/July). Imperial College, London's RE-ACT SURVEY, estimated that infections doubled every six days. On 7 July, 32,548 positive tests were reported, the highest daily figure since 24 January. If the epidemic was doubling every six days, there would be more than 100,000 a day by 19 July. Another 33 deaths were reported, and 386 hospital admissions were up 44% in one week. The study also found that one in 70 people tested positive for the virus between 24 June and 5 July.

However, infection rates were three times lower among the fully vaccinated and were mainly confined to younger adults. Men were 30% more likely to test positive for COVID-19 than women. Experts believe this was due to them gathering indoors to watch football.

Allowing virus cases to rise is a significant risk, and restrictions may need to return this winter. Even if hospitalisations and deaths remain relatively low, major risks still exist in allowing cases to surge. SAGE, the government's 'Scientific Advisory Group for Emergencies', believe that should a 'variant of concern' arrive that threatened immunity, lockdown restrictions would need to be reimposed for much longer.

Infections have been on the increase since January and are likely to reach 50,000 a day within weeks. Consequently, hospitalisations and deaths will increase. SAGE's assessment of long-term measures for dealing with the epidemic was that keeping some level of measures in place both through summer and beyond would significantly decrease ongoing transmission. The latest data (6 July) shows that infections are up 53% in one week, and 27,334 cases and nine deaths have been recorded in the UK. Nine in ten adults now have COVID antibodies as the vaccine roll-out pushes Britain close to 'herd immunity'. Blood testing by the ONS found that 89.8% of over 16s in England have some immunity to the virus. This is an increase from 79.6% one month ago, reflecting the success of the vaccine programme.

Antibody levels were highest in older adults, with 97% of those between 60 and 79 testing positive. However, only six in ten of those aged 16 to 24 tested positive. This means millions of younger adults remain susceptible to the virus. However, this data also suggests the UK may be approaching 'herd immunity'. Experts believe that around 85% of the total population of the UK require antibodies to reach this 'immunity threshold'. The latest data from the ONS suggests that currently, one in 160 people have the COVID virus. This is an increase from one in 250 in the previous week. The Delta variant now accounts for 99% of all confirmed cases.

At 8 July, the total confirmed COVID-19 cases was 5,022,893, with total deaths at 128,336. People in hospital with the virus numbered 2,636. Between 1 and 7 July, 192.902 people were confirmed positive for the virus, an increase of 42.8% from the previous week. 33 deaths were registered on 7 July, and between 1 and 7 July, 161 deaths were recorded.

Hospital admissions for COVID have started to drop after weekly cases declined by up to 38%. The number of patients being hospitalised in the UK has also fallen, indicating that the epidemic is past its peak. On 28 July, 27,734 cases were recorded, an increase of 18% on the previous day. Daily cases have averaged 30,494 over seven days, compared to 47,695 the previous week. Approximately 825 patients have been admitted with COVID, down from 854 the previous day. Deaths are at 91, down from 131. The success of the vaccine roll-out now means that the death rate is now a tenth of what it was in previous waves.

COVID–19 Statistical Time-Line: 2020/2021
28 February 2020: First case of COVID-19 reported in the UK.
Week ending 7 March: cases increase to 77.
Week ending 14 March: Cases stand at 1,543, with 55 deaths recorded.
9 April: Highest daily deaths at 938.
14 May: Survey suggests one in 400 infected with COVID -19.
First week of June: Deaths increased to 40,000.
10 August: Decrease in confirmed cases by 90%, deaths reduced by 5,000.
By end of August, estimated that approximately 3-4 million people in England had COVID-19.
Week beginning 1st October, UK reported 22,961 cases and by the end of that month, this had surged to 1 million cases.

By the middle of November 2020, infection rates stopped increasing across England, and the 'R' rate was below 1. The highest infection rates were among those aged

20-29, estimated at 362.1 per 100,000 population on 15 November. There was a slight increase in positive cases in people aged 70-79 (147.5 per 100,000) and those over 80 (to 245.3 per 100,000). Increases were also observed in those aged 10-19 to 257.4 per 100,000. Hospital admissions were down to 15.5 per 100,000. By the week ending 22 November, there were 633,000 confirmed cases of COVID.

By the end of December 2020, 39,237 positive tests were confirmed, with the 'R' number estimated at 1.5. During December, there were 20,917 COVID-19 patients in hospital in the UK. 744 deaths were registered during the month. The 'Kent' or Alpha variant was identified. Between 27 December 2020 and 2 January 2021, one in 50 had been infected with COVID. The overall infection rate had risen by 70% in the final two weeks of December. London was the worst-affected area, with an estimated one in 30 infected. Hospitals in London had more than 6,800 in-patients. The ONS figures showed that 31.2% of registered deaths in the last week of December had symptoms of COVID. These amounted to 3,144.

On 1 January 2021, there were 10,069 deaths registered in England and Wales. On 5 January, an all-time high was seen with 60,916 positive tests and 830 deaths registered. Hospital admissions stood at 3,351. By the 16th of the month, 3,569 hospital admissions were recorded – down from a peak of 4,134 on 12 January. On 18 January, there were 30,846 in hospital and 599 COVID-linked deaths. On 25 January, there were 2,648 admitted to hospital, and by 28 January, this had risen to 39,249.

By 2 March, there were 4,188,400 confirmed cases of COVID in the UK and 123,296 registered deaths. In the first week of April, it was estimated that one in 1,000 people over 65 years tested positive. By the week ending 23 April, one in 40 deaths were linked to COVID. On 27 April, there were 1,310 patients in hospital, a decrease of 96% from the record number of 30,846 on 18 January. The total deaths recorded in April were 38,899, 6.1% below the five-year April average. The overall mortality rate for COVID in April was 20.6 per 100,000 population – one in 5,000.

By the final week of May, cases began to increase by 4,000, and the 'R' rate was above 1 for the first time since mid-January. By 28 May, the total cases for the month were 4,182, with an average daily increase of 24%. By the week ending 28 May, there had been 93 deaths. On 1 June, there were no coronavirus deaths recorded, and for the early part of the month, the daily deaths averaged 6 per day. The deaths since the beginning of the pandemic stood at 127,782. At the January peak, daily deaths stood at 1,820.

By 2 June, there were 776 patients in hospital. In early June, one in every 125 deaths were linked to COVID, but by 11 June, symptoms of the virus were present in only 0.8% of people dying in that week. 14 times as many deaths were attributed to 'flu and pneumonia' than COVID during June.

Across the UK, the number of deaths registered in the week ending 11 June was 11,66, of which just 93 were COVID-linked. Between the start of the pandemic in 2020 and 11 June 2021, there were 132,434 COVID-linked deaths recorded in England and 7,897 in Wales.

On 1 July, 26,068 new cases were reported, with daily hospitalisations at 263 – an increase of 6.4%. The figures for hospital admissions were 1,720, compared to 7,000 in 2020. Deaths and hospitalisations increased by 10%.

On 7 July, 32,548 positive tests were recorded – the highest daily figure since 24 January. There were 33 deaths registered on that day and 386 hospital admissions. This was an increase of 44%. Between 24 June and 5 August, one in 170 tested positive for the virus.

Data for 8 July 2021 suggests that (at the time of writing), one in 160 people have COVID. The Delta variant now accounts for 99% of confirmed cases. The total confirmed cases are 5,022, 893 with total deaths at 128,336 as of 8 July 2021. In-patients in hospital are at 2,636. Between 1 and 7 July, 161 deaths were recorded, an increase of 42.5% over the previous week.

Statistical Data

COVID-19: Confirmed Positive Cases February 2020 to July 2021

2020	
19 February	9
1 March	35
1 April	26,662
1 May	160,477
1 June	249,891
1 July	283,486
1 August	303,399
1 September	339,792
1 October	475,305
1 November	1,033,021
1 December	1,640,019
2021	
1 January	2,536,128
1 February	3,824,945
1 March	4,169,164
1 April	4,334,546
1 May	4,408,715
1 June	4,486,953
8 July	5,022,893

COVID–19 Deaths

March 2020 to 8 July 2021

2020	
5 March	1
1 April	3,089
1 May	27,363
1 June	37,582
1 July	40,643
1 August	41,255
1 September	41,557
1 October	42,321
1 November	46,771
1 December	59,126
2021	
I January	74,669
1 February	106,714
1 March	123,125
1 April	126,764
1 May	127,524
1 June	127,782
8 July	128,336

Source: worldometers-covid-19/data/uk

Deaths By Age Range and Presence of Pre-Conditions

Between 1 January and 9 April 2021

Age	Pre-Cond %	No Pre-Cond %	Male %	Female %
0-19	0.04	0.01	0.02	0.03
20-39	0.54	0.09	0.27	0.36
40-59	6.06	0.68	2.42	4.33
60-79	36.09	1.70	13.38	24.53
80+	53.04	1.63	23.67	30.99

Hospital Admissions

From 1-28 January 2021
Under 65:   39%
65 and Over: 60%

From 16 May-12 June 2021
Under 65:   70%
65 and Over: 30%

Deaths by Place of Occurrence

2020 – First Wave: 13 March to 4 September 2020

Home	Hospital	Hospice	Care Home	Other
2,306	31,033	717	14,720	402
4.7%	63.1%	1.5%	29.9%	0.8%

Total deaths over period: 49,178

2020/21– Second Wave: 11 September to 1 January 2021

Home	Hospital	Hospice	Care Home	Other
1,338	20,049	340	4, 732	145
5.0%	75.4%	1.3%	17.8%	0.6%

Total deaths over period: 26,604

2021 – 2 January to 2 April

Home	Hospital	Hospice	Care Home	Other
3,792	39,056	983	11,051	778
6.9%	70.6%	1.8%	20%	0.7%

Total deaths over period: 55,660

Source: ons.gov.uk/coronavirus data

Estimates of the 'R' Number in the UK at 8 July 2021

England	1.1 to 1.3
Scotland	1.2 to 1.5
Wales	1.1 to 1.4
Northern Ireland	1.2 to 1.6

Estimates of the 'R' Number by English Regions

East England	1.0 to 1.2
London	1.0 to 1.2
Midlands	1.2 to 1.3
North East & Yorkshire	1.2 to 1.4
North West	1.0 to 1.3
South East	1.1 to 1.3
South West	1.3 to 1.6

Vaccinations Across English Regions at 23 June 2021

Region	**% First Dose**	**% Second Dose**
South West	76	59
North East	75	56
East Midlands	75	57
South East	74	55
East England	74	55
Yorks & Humber	73	55
North West	73	54
West Midlands	71	54
London	58	37

Vaccine Take-Up Among Ethnic Minorities

Percentage Vaccinated By Age Group

Ages	80+	70-79	65-69	60-64
White	98	97	95	93
S. Asian	88	88	87	86
Mixed	84	83	80	78
Other	84	81	77	75
Black	76	74	71	69

Ages	55-59	50-54
White	92	89
S. Asian	84	81
Mixed	75	73
Other	73	70
Black	66	64

UK Vaccinations at 8 July 2021:

Population having had at least 1 dose   45,697,87
68.6%

Population fully vaccinated (both doses)   34,374,246
51.6%

Source: ons.gov.uk/coronavirusdata

Chapter Five: Reflections

This final chapter comprises a diverse collection of commentaries that have appeared in the *Daily Mail* throughout the coronavirus pandemic in England. The authors all have had direct or indirect experience of the progress of the pandemic by virtue of their respective professional work.

These commentaries are wide-ranging in their content and have been submitted by scientists, medical experts, sociologists, economists and established media correspondents. Their views are personal, and some may appear controversial, but all are based on sound reasoning, reflecting the writer's perceptions of the pandemic. These are both revealing and thought-provoking, providing the reader with a balanced overview of the impact COVID-19 has had on England's social and economic life.

It is anticipated that the reader will find these commentaries of value in arriving at their conclusions regarding the British government's response to the unprecedented threat posed by the Coronavirus pandemic.

Commentary – The Cure is Worse Than the Disease

"The supposed cure for Coronavirus is turning out to be worse than the disease. As analysis by the Mail reveals today, more lives are being wrecked by the official response to COVID than by the virus itself. In a bizarre paradox, ill-directed efforts at protecting public health are creating a public health disaster. When the outbreak began, the Government decided to shield the NHS, with the aim of maintaining its capacity for the imminent tidal wave of cases. All resources were focussed on this goal. From March, the treatment of other conditions and illnesses was put in abeyance for three months. And to this day, the NHS has not resumed anything like normal service. But the predicted COVID deluge never materialised. Even now the fiercely disputed current COVID death toll of 41,628 is barely half the total fatalities of the 1968 flu epidemic in the UK. Yet the impact of COVID has been truly devastating in a much more insidious way. As today's figures reveal, the effective suspension of much of the NHS, and the mass deferral of non-COVID cases, have wreaked havoc on the nation's health. Hospital admissions for cancer were down by 36 per cent in April and another 37 per cent in May. As a doctor who served as director of cancer services in Rotherham for over 12 years, I feel despair at these statistics. For ultimately they are proof that this crisis has warped the Government's and medical authorities' senses of reality, purpose and compassion.

In my field of cancer, NHS guidelines give patients who show any potentially cancerous symptoms – such as a persistent cough, sudden weight loss or blood in the stool, a legal right to be seen by a specialist within two weeks of an urgent GP referral. Diagnosis should be made within 28 days and, if needed, 95 per cent of patients should begin treatment within 62 days from the original referral. But in the post-COVID climate of severe healthcare rationing, this target has simply been abandoned. One member of my family who found blood in their urine had to wait more than three and a half months just to be seen. Tragically, the whole point of cancer pathways is to catch the disease early before it advances and spreads. Yet that basic medical requirement has been ignored in the obsessive attention paid to coronavirus. And so the very ministers and public health bureaucrats who constantly claimed to be 'saving lives' have put numerous lives at risk with their distorted priorities. Due to wilful neglect, the damage caused to cancer patients will be felt for years to come. The same applies to so many other conditions, including cardiovascular problems, diabetes, mental health and dementia where patients have been denied timely care. Of course, it is not just delayed treatment that is to blame. The draconian lock-down, now in its second incarnation, also fuels poor health by the harm it inflicts on the economy – through poverty and unemployment – as well as putting people in enforced isolation.

It is a tragic fact, as history demonstrates, higher suicide rates invariably follow declines in a nation's GDP, particularly among the young – those least likely to suffer from COVID. As for the elderly, who are most vulnerable to COVID, in another bitter irony, they are the ones who suffer most from the latest restrictions introduced today, the 'Rule of Six' guidelines. Every doctor knows that life can never be about simply the avoidance of death: it's also about the quality of life. Yet, too many older people have been forced to endure a kind of solitary confinement, denied ordinary pleasures such as contact with friends, hugs from grandchildren, or local outings. Even more cruel is the arbitrary rule that only one relative at a time can be at the bedside of a loved one, even in their final moments. Tearing families apart, denying them comfort at the end, COVID authoritarianism generates the antithesis of compassionate care. All of which makes it all the more frustrating that this callous, illiberal approach is built on such shallow foundations. There is precious little evidence that Coronavirus was ever an exceptional threat to our nation's well being. In effect, the State has wildly over-reacted, partly as a result of being in thrall to scientists such as Professor Neil Ferguson with unproven theories and dubious modelling. Despite the Government's misplaced talk about the dangerous consequences of a 'second wave', the reality is that the rising number of infections – the inevitable result of greatly increased testing – has not clearly resulted in a significant increase in COVID hospital admission or deaths.

More than 1,600 people die in Britain every day, yet, despite the Government's scaremongering, the Coronavirus daily death toll has been in single or low double figures for weeks. Indeed, if coronavirus were really the deadly menace that is painted, there would have been a massive spike in cases and deaths after the Black Lives Matter protests, illegal raves and huge gatherings at the seaside during the summer. But nothing of the sort has happened. Yet, still the Government refuses to change its doom-laden narrative. On the contrary, the bullying is becoming more intense, reflected in the appointment of COVID marshals and the ritualistic orders to wear masks. The great Irish author CS Lewis wrote that "of all tyrannies, a tyranny sincerely exercised for the good of its victims may be the most oppressive. It would be better to live under robber barons than omnipotent moral busybodies". As this country finally faces up to the real healthcare toll of imposing lock-down, such words could have been describing Britain in 2020".

The Author, Dr John Lee, is a former professor of pathology at Hull York Medical School, and a recently retired NHS consultant., Daily Mail, 14 September 2020, page 7.

Commentary – A Blind Refusal to see Sense

"The greatest weapon we possess in the battle against COVID-19 is the evidence accumulated by scientists. Although this is a new disease, essentially unknown a year ago, we have gathered a vast amount of data on it. No other disease in history has been so intensely studied by so many people around the world over such a concentrated period, both in the lab and in the real world. Yet the British government appears to be paying far less attention to this vital evidence than it should be. The statement to the Commons earlier this week by the Health Secretary Matt Hancock, was largely preoccupied instead with the overall number of cases. This headline figure is misleading, COVID-19 does not affect all people equally. For the majority, it is a comparatively innocuous infection that many young people will have without symptoms. For the vulnerable minority, especially the elderly, it can be very serious. In the over-80s, in fact, the mortality rate is as high as it was for smallpox before the introduction of vaccines, more than two centuries ago. That is to say, for patients in that group, COVID-19 is a very grave threat indeed. Government policy, such as the introduction of a nightlife curfew yesterday, seems blind to this crucial difference. It concentrates simply on reducing the blanket figure, without making the vulnerable a priority. This approach lacks common sense and seems to be driven solely by a fear of red bars on graphs. That is why about 30 scientific experts and I signed a letter to the Prime Minister and his advisers this week, calling for a targeted approach that is based on evidence.

At the forefront of this approach should be how we handle the crisis in care homes. At the start of the pandemic, the disease was allowed to run rampant in homes for the elderly, and the result was many thousands of preventable deaths. It is no exaggeration to call this a national scandal of massive proportions. The crisis is still not fully under control. Care homes should be at the apex of protective controls. Above all, the policy ought to focus on ensuring COVID-19 does not get into the homes in the first place. The only effective way to do that is by consistent, reliable testing with quick results. It is impracticable to expect carers, who work with very elderly residents, many of whom have dementia, to use full PPE or protective equipment. The patients might well fail to understand what is happening, and be frightened. It is also impossible to do this care work while maintaining social distance. Physical contact is an integral part of the job. All the emphasis should be on frequent testing, to make sure carers can be confident they are not carrying the virus. Yet we are hearing next to nothing from government ministers about this. Most of our hospitals are not working at anything close to capacity. People are staying away as much as they can, believing both that they should leave the NHS to get on with handling COVID-19 cases, and that hospitals are hotbeds for infection. Yet these are both misconceptions.

Serious illnesses including heart disease and cancer are being missed, because people are too scared to report their symptoms or get a screening. As a result, lives are being lost. Already the data shows that unnecessary death or 'excess mortality' is on the rise. The Government's chief aim appears to be keeping the overall number of COVID-19 cases as low as possible, until a vaccine can be released. Even by the most optimistic projection, this will not happen before next year, and a vaccination programme will bring its own problems. Because multiple vaccines are being trialled and tested, the Government will face a difficult choice over which one to implement. Worse, because this jab will be fast-tracked into use, it will be hard to assess how safe it is, or how good it is at stemming infections. Even the best vaccines won't work unless they are applied across a large majority of the population. We already know from opinion polls that a substantial proportion of people will baulk at having a largely untried COVID-19 vaccine. Especially as virtually all under-40s wouldn't need one for their own personal health, we'd be asking millions of people to have a jab for purely altruistic reasons, to protect others. I want to be optimistic, but vaccines will not be the silver bullet that ends the pandemic. Waiting is pointless. We have to act now and be practical. That means focusing on protecting the vulnerable, most of all in our care homes, with effective testing. This is the crucial aspect we must get right. Shutting down the country is a dangerous distraction."

The author, Hugh Pennington, is Emeritus Professor of Bacteriology at the University of Aberdeen. Daily Mail, 23 September 2020, Page 13.

Commentary – Why Britain Must Not Be Sacrificed On The Altar Of Fighting COVID

"Boris Johnson, it emerged this week, has finally decided to disagree with Sage, the committee of scientists that seems to have been running our response to the pandemic ever since it became clear we had an international crisis on our hands. They have recommended the return of a full national lock-down of the sort imposed in March on a temporary basis to halt the spread of the virus. Such a step would have meant the wholesale suspension of the hospitality trade, closure of outlets such as gyms and hairdressers and a ban on household mixing. Their advocacy of this so-called 'circuit breaker' shows how some members of the scientific community have lost their sense of proportion. In essence, they want the entire well-being of the nation sacrificed on the altar of the fight against COVID. But it ignores the devastating social and economic impact of COVID restrictions, and exaggerates the threat the disease poses. Of course we must seek to save the lives of those seriously affected by the coronavirus, but we must not be so narrow minded as to forget people suffering from other conditions and the catastrophic effect of our approach on the economy. Here are the key issues lock-down advocates must take on board, and on which there has been a deafening silence from some of our leaders.

Death Rates Are Remarkably Low

Despite all the hysteria, this is not a modern plague. In the week ending October 2, COVID accounted for just 3.2 per cent of all fatalities in British hospitals. Even with the recent rise in infections, COVID mortality levels are drastically lower now than at the peak of the pandemic in the spring. On April 8, according to the Office for National Statistics, 975 people died with COVID, compared to 74 last Wednesday. Similarly, in the week ending April 17,

8,758 fatalities were recorded that mentioned COVID-19 as a possible factor on the death certificate. For the first week in October, that figure was just 321. That toll may increase, but it is highly unlikely to reach the levels we saw in spring.

Disease Of The Old And Vulnerable

COVID-19 is a cruel disease that targets the old or those whose life expectancy is compromised by ill-health. While every life is precious, the average age of patients who die with COVID-19 is 82.4. Since August, just one otherwise healthy person under 30 has died with the disease, while in the same period only 97 victims have been younger than 60. One study in June by the Office for National Statistics found 91 per cent of people who died with COVID in England and Wales between March and June had at least one pre-existing condition. This is not to trivialise the virus. Every life is valuable, but COVID-19 deaths are no more or less important than any others.

Better Outcomes

As knowledge of COVID-19 has deepened, so survival rates have improved significantly. Drugs such as remdesivir and dexamethasone are highly effective in treating the disease, while it is now recognised ventilators can sometimes do more harm than good. For those admitted to intensive care with COVID, the chances of survival have gone up to 80 per cent. Even for the very elderly, contracting it need not be a death sentence. Contrary to the depressing propaganda, six in every seven people who are infected over the age of 90 actually survive.

Grim Warnings Go Unrealised

In their controversial press briefing on September 21, just before the imposition of new pub curfews and rules on mask-wearing, Chief Medical Officer Chris Whitty and Chief Scientific Adviser Sir Patrick Vallance warned Britain could have 50,000 new daily infections by mid-October. Though they stressed it was not 'a prediction', but 'an illustration', of what could happen without action, they offered no alternative scenario. Yet we have reached mid-October and their grim warning has, thankfully, been unfilled. Over the past week, the rate of infections has averaged 14,000.

Little To Back Pub And Bar Closures

Targeting the hospitality trade, the mix of curfews and closures has been central to the Government's anti-COVID strategy. But in truth there is little convincing scientific evidence to support the belief that these venues are significant arena of transmission. This is confirmed by Sage papers, released on Monday which accepted the economic damage of closures outweighs any potential health benefits.

Lock-Downs Don't Work

Much of the North and the Midlands has been living with COVID restrictions for months, yet it has not stemmed the rise in positive cases. Revealingly, Chris Whitty stated at Monday's briefing that he did not think even the most extreme Tier 3 crackdown – now imposed in Liverpool – would have much impact. Much of the momentum behind the recent increase has been driven by the return of students to universities without symptoms – only to be mass tested and told they are infected. But young people are those in least danger. There is not a single documented case of any student this autumn dying from COVID. Given these low risks, it might be counter-productive to curb infections among students since, by contracting the disease, they can boost immunity in their communities.

Hunt For A Vaccine

Yearning for release from the cycle of COVID despair, the public have been encouraged by the Government to pin its hopes on a vaccine. But such faith may be misplaced. The task is not easy. In 40 years, scientists have never found an HIV/AIDS vaccine, nor has one been discovered for the SARS virus in 18 years. Second, a vaccine may not be a panacea. It will probably be more like an annual flu jab – which will give some protection but not stop you contracting the disease – rather than a measles vaccine, which provides a lifetime's protection. We shall probably have to learn to live with the virus, with nearly all of us infected at some point. Last week a report by Edinburgh University argued that heavy-handed use of lock-downs and social distancing could cost between 149,000 and 178,000 lives over the course of the pandemic – far more than have died from COVID – by preventing the establishment of herd immunity.

Economic Disaster

The economic damage caused by lock-downs, curfews and restrictions is becoming even more apparent. We now face a winter of lengthening dole queues, growing poverty, and mass business failure. Even with Rishi Sunak's Eat Out to Help Out Scheme, August growth was sluggish. Only yesterday it was revealed that redundancies in the three months to the end of August jumped by 114,000, while between March and September the number of people claiming out-of-work benefits rose 120 per cent to 2.7 million. And the soaring public debt – with the Government likely borrowing more than £350 billion this year – will have to be paid by generations to come.

The Wider Impact

The wreckage to the economy will worsen physical and mental health. Depression, family breakdown and suicide look certain to rise. Because of the relentless narrow focus by authorities on COVID, other medical conditions are badly neglected. Oncologists warn there could be 50,000 premature deaths from cancer, due to deferred treatments and diagnostic screening failures. The same pattern is found with other health problems, made worse by a reluctance to attend hospital for fear of being a burden – or contracting COVID. It's time for a wider range of ideas and voices to be heard. The question we need to ask is: how can we make this transition to living with the virus, rather than be traumatised by a futile fight against it?"

The author, Robert Dingwall, is professor of sociology at Nottingham Trent University, and a member of groups advising the Government on the pandemic. He is writing in a personal capacity. Daily Mail, 14 October 2020.

Commentary – Nothing Would Fuel Anti-Vaxx Madness More Than Insisting On 'Jab Passports'

"Amid the wintery gloom, a series of new vaccines have been justifiably hailed as the breakthrough against coronavirus. With Britain having ordered 357 million doses of seven different vaccines, at last there is real hope that the depressing cycle of lock-down and contagion could be broken next year. Yet, as the *Mail* reported yesterday, into this optimistic scene has stepped Nadhim Zahawi, the minister responsible for vaccines, to indicate that some venues-such as sports stadiums, restaurants, cinemas and pubs-may insist on proof of vaccination to grant people entry. This would be a profoundly dangerous and un-British move. Heavy-handedness and authoritarianism have characterised much of this Government's approach during the pandemic, from the pub curfew to the rule of six, ordering people to wear masks in shops and restricting travel and access to their loved ones. But now a potential instrument of salvation – a vaccine – must not be allowed to be turned into a weapon of state surveillance.

According to Mr Zahawi, so-called 'immunity passports' would enable customers to provide proof that they 'have been vaccinated'. He added blandly, 'We will make the technology as easy and accessible as possible'. Yesterday, as anger grew about this potential new system, Cabinet Office Minister Michael Gove used a BBC interview to adopt a more sceptical tone. 'Let's not get ahead of ourselves: that's not the plan' he insisted. But nor did Mr Gove issue a denial. Moreover, given this Government's record of vacillations, inconsistencies and policy reversals, it is easy to imagine that another U-turn could be made.

Let me be clear: a vaccine 'passport' would be a disaster – not only for basic freedom, but for public health, too. It would be wrong in principle and wrong in practice. As well as being a gross invasion of personal privacy even on a limited basis, there is a clear risk of a slippery slope. Once established to arbitrate entry to cinemas and pubs, the use of these passports could be endlessly extended. Those without them could end up being denied access to holiday travel, public transport and universities – and even healthcare, social security and certain jobs. Indeed, Australia already has a 'no jab, no pay' law, where parents who refuse to get their children vaccinated become ineligible for child and tax benefits. It is a small step from there towards full, mandatory immunisation, as currently exists in parts of Europe. France, Germany and Italy all make certain vaccinations compulsory (in Italy, for example, immunisation against diphtheria, polio and tetanus are all mandatory). This is a reflection of the historic continental attachment to the powerful state – as well as to voluble anti-vaxxer sentiment in those countries. But that is not the tradition here. In the land that created Magna Carta, pioneered parliamentary democracy and defeated Nazi tyranny, respect for liberty runs deep.

Barred from the pub, the football stadium, the aircraft, who would feel able to refuse a jab? This compulsory vaccination by the backdoor would be another huge advance towards the Big Brother state, complete with a vast new database, extensive bureaucracy, bossy officialdom and endless regulations. Mr Zahawi says that the scheme may be needed to send 'a very strong message' that this is 'good for your family, good for your community and good for your country'. But the law is not meant to be a vehicle for propaganda. Instead of plotting to use threats and coercion, the Government should be resorting to persuasion, trying to reassure the public about about safety and seeking to convince people that it is in their own interests to have a jab. That is also the way to deal with the anti-vaccination movement, which thrives on wild conspiracy theories. Although I respect the fundamental right of the anti-vaxxers to protest, I reject their irresponsible gospel of delusion and fear. In fact, all my children have had their necessary jabs, and I am sure my family will join the COVID vaccination programme when it reaches us.

But the biggest possible boost would be given to the anti-vaxxers cause if the Government went down the mandatory path, even by default. Such a policy would not only feed all their paranoia about the big state, but would give them a new pretext for martyrdom. In a climate of confrontation, public anxieties would be heightened, making any passport scheme counterproductive. There are a host of other practical problems. Businesses, battered by COVID, may be reluctant to act as agents of officialdom. A passport scheme might also backfire and encourage reckless or illicit activity. Underground, passport-free venues will operate in the shadows, while a black market will develop in forged immunity certificates. Furthermore, from the loss of computer discs to the sale of personal information, the state has an appalling recent record on protecting sensitive data. Nor will the over-stretched police have the resources to crack down on infringements accelerating contempt for the law- and endangering public health.

There is also ethical questions. Some people may have legitimate health reasons for having to refuse the jab, yet in society where immunisation becomes the key to participation, they may be stigmatised, even ostracised. It would be a catastrophe if we in Britain began to build a social structure based on a bureaucratic evaluation of each individual's health. Mr Zahawi claimed on Monday that an immunity scheme 'is the way we return to whole country to normal'. But a Britain of identity databases and demands to see papers can never be 'normal'. On the contrary, it will be a deeply sinister, alien place where the flag of freedom will fly low. Rather than embarking down this road, the Government would do far better to concentrate all of its energies on a successful roll-out programme. This is a daunting enough challenge, requiring vast numbers of volunteers to administer the actual doses of vaccine. Against the backdrop of PPE and testing fiascos, the Government's record of establishing immunisation centres and supplies of everything from glass vials to syringes and their record on logistics is hardly impressive. Ministers had better get it right this time, and that means they should avoid dreaming up grim fantasies about state bullying.

Earlier this week, Boris Johnson described the hope generated by the vaccines. 'The armies of science are coming to our aid,' he said, 'with all the morale-boosting, bugle-blasting excitement of Wellington's Prussian allies coming through the woods on the afternoon of Waterloo'. Let us hope that we do not end up with another Teutonic import: the feared secret police of socialist East Germany, known as the Stasi, demanding to see our papers".

The author, Laura Perrins, is a former barrister and co-editor of The Conservative Woman website. Daily Mail, 2 December 2020, Page 22.

Commentary – When Will They Learn The Terrible Lesson Of Locking Our Children Out Of Their Schools?

"For secondary pupils, the announcement yesterday that many schools may not open fully until the February half-term holiday is a cruel and deeply unnecessary blow. I fear hundreds of thousands of young people will spend the rest of their lives paying for this disastrous decision, foisted on the Government by callous and opportunistic unions bent on exploiting the pandemic for political advantage. As a school governor and former teacher, I am furious at the news that, while primary schools are open after the Christmas holidays and pupils studying for GCSEs and A-levels in Years 11 and 13 will be able to return to class, the rest face weeks of more inadequate online learning. The damage done to their progress is already catastrophic and probably irreparable. Despite a general reopening last September, many schools have not been functioning fully since March. We are a long way past the point where extra homework can fill in the gaps. A single day when classrooms are closed means more than the loss of just one day's education. Every teacher knows that lessons are about reinforcing knowledge, going back over the ground already covered to make sure facts are firmly planted. If lessons are not instilled daily, many children will slide backwards. It now looks as though, on average, secondary students are between 15 months and 22 months behind the point where we would expect them to be. Put it plainly, 12-year-olds in Year 8 have slipped back to the level they were at when they moved up from primary school. And in some cases, they have regressed still further. All their secondary progress has been lost. It's unthinkable, but true. And it's not happening in just a few isolated classrooms – this is the story all over the country. Such a statement might sound melodramatic. But it is based on reliable evidence. Of course, I recognise that the Government has to listen to scientific health advisers who are monitoring the spread of coronavirus. But I am frustrated beyond belief that no attention is being paid to other scientific evidence that measures the educational cost of lock-down for schools and pupils. Does anyone in the cabinet think it's acceptable for pupils to be 22 months behind? What do they imagine will be the outcome for this generation?

It's so brutally unfair to load the greatest burden onto the young. We're all suffering from the restrictions – cut off from our friends and wider family, our jobs are at risk, the threat of swingeing tax rises to come. However, no one is paying a higher price than schoolchildren. It is not only their daily lives and friendships that are being turned upside down, but their whole futures. Without education, their prospects are permanently harmed.

The ground is lost that can never be regained. Inevitably, it is pupils from disadvantaged backgrounds who are worst-hit. It's deeply unrealistic to imagine that children from families in the lowest economic bracket will be able to carry on learning via laptop. Even if there were enough portable computers to go round (and believe me there are not), many children don't have access to reliable broadband. I know of children who have to resort to piggybacking on their neighbour's internet signal to download learning materials. In homes where for example, there is one computer between three children of different ages, constant tensions arise over who has access and when.

Pressures are exacerbated when adults in the house are trying to use the wi-fi to work from home. The cases I know about are just in London, but I'm sure the same problems are repeated in different ways across rural Britain where internet speeds are often inadequate. Yet none of this is taken into account when the Government says blithely that pupils will have to 'continue learning from home'. You might as well cancel the school bus and tell children that in future they can flap their arms and fly. It reveals an utter lack of practical thinking. The suggestion by union leaders that schools should remain closed to allow more time to prepare for COVID testing and protective measures is particularly mendacious. Schools up and down Britain have made exceptional efforts to ensure their environments are as safe as humanly possible. Social distancing restrictions are enforced everywhere. Corridors are run on a rigid one-way system, hygiene rules are meticulously enforced and battalions of cleaners have been drafted in. To pretend that another few weeks will enable these measures to be upgraded is false. They are as good as they can possibly get. Everyone understands the importance of driving down infection rates and ensuring the NHS is not overloaded. But it is also an inescapable fact that young children, adolescents and teenagers are the least likely to be seriously affected by this virus. In the majority of cases, those with the infection won't even know they've got it – they will have no symptoms and experience no illness. Why then must they bear the brunt of COVID restrictions? Why are their lives being ruined? How do we imagine that we can ever compensate them for their ruined education?

On top of all this, the parents of pupils who cannot now return to class must be tearing their hair out in despair. I am very strongly of the opinion that teachers are not childminders and schools do not exist to get children out of the house. However, there is a practical aspect here and when class rooms are empty then millions of parents will be struggling to do their jobs. That's very difficult for individual families, where wages may be suddenly curtailed. Moreover, it is disastrous for the national economy. Society is a machine of complex interconnections and it is currently at a standstill.

Take one vital cog out of the engine and the wheels start to seize up. Make no mistake – there are militants in the teaching unions who want this to happen. They see this as an opportunity to wreak social havoc and perhaps bring down the Government. This is about extremist politics and has nothing to do with education. The children are treated as expendable pawns. Do not blame the teachers for the actions of their unions. In most cases, they probably haven't been consulted or offered any kind of ballot. Not everyone is held hostage by the unions. The headteachers I talk to regularly are planning to open as normal, as are many around the country. Most teachers are desperate to get back to the job they love. It's crucial that the Government backs them. Downing Street has to resist the urge to capitulate.

Schools have to open for all our children. Undermining their young lives is not the way to beat coronavirus."
The author, Calvin Robinson, is a school governor and former teacher.
Daily Mail, 29 December 2020, Page 5.

Commentary – Senseless Fines Will Only Foster Contempt

"We all know we are in the middle of a pandemic, that COVID-19 is spread by human contact, that the new strain of the virus is significantly more infectious, that cases are soaring and deaths are high – and that the NHS is in danger of being overwhelmed. We know too, that we all have a responsibility to keep contact with others to a bare minimum. It is dangerous and wrong to hold parties, raves and other gatherings – and quite right for the police to use their powers to break them up. But there comes a point at which over-zealous enforcement of the rules becomes dangerous in itself. If we want everyone to obey the lock-down rules it is vital that those rules have public consent. Lose this and we find ourselves in a situation which tends to afflict all dictatorships after a while – where people pay lip service to laws but have such contempt for the rules that they are determined to break them at every opportunity. Moreover, it destroys public trust even further when police are seen apparently making up the law as they go along. As the National Police Chief's Council has since acknowledged, there is nothing in the legislation passed last week that prevents someone driving five miles to take a socially distanced walk in the country. This is exactly what the two women stopped at a Derbyshire reservoir last week had done – they went there, they said, because it was less crowded than the paths near their homes. The tea they had taken to drink on a bitter day apparently constituted a 'picnic', and they were fined £200 each on the vague grounds of breaking the 'spirit' of lock-down.

Nor is there anything in the legislation to prevent people leaving their home twice a day – the 'offence' over

which an overly 'keen' Thames Valley policeman chal-
lenged drivers following the new national lock-down. The
'once-a-day' rule is a guideline, but it is not law. The Home
Secretary Priti Patel and Health Secretary Matt Hancock
surely knew that, so why were they so keen yesterday to
jump to the support of police officers who appear to have
acted outside the powers that Parliament voted to give
them? The irony is that the only social interaction likely to
spread COVID is any of these instances was between police officers and the people they were tackling for per-
ceived breaches of lock-down. Do these crowds of police
hanging around the streets possess some kind of immunity
to the disease which the rest of us do not? I am sure that the
vast majority of officers around the country are not acting
disproportionately, but are enforcing the rules with common sense – giving advice and verbal warnings to people
who, in many cases, are simply confused by the ever-chan-
ging rules.

But it damages the reputation of the police as a
whole when some start behaving like the Stasi. I wonder
whether those individuals who've been interrogated by
over-zealous boys in blue in recent days will be inclined to
cooperate with officers in future if, for example, their assistance is required as witnesses to a real crime? And I find
it particularly worrying that several cases seem to have involved crowds of male officers surrounding women who
are either alone or in pairs. It is as if years of equality training have gone out of the window and some officers suddenly think themselves entitled to pick on what they see as
soft targets. We all need to follow the rules of lock-down,
but that will be made easier if police forces can retain our
respect by acting proportionately, rather than jumping on
the first person they can find an excuse to fine."
Author, Ross Clark, Daily Mail, 11 January 2021, Page 5.

Commentary – Why Gaffes And Unhealthy Ageing Nation Are To Blame

Delays and Mistakes

"There is no doubt the government has made many mistakes. The prime minister was far too slow to order lock-down last spring. Studies have shown ordering restrictions a few days earlier would have potentially saved tens of thousands of lives, although Boris Johnson's reluctance to shut the economy in March was perhaps understandable given the unprecedented nature of the crisis. Testing at the start of the pandemic was grossly inadequate. Failure to stop the virus being imported from abroad – ironic, given Mr Johnson was elected on a pledge to take back control of the nation's borders – has also been instrumental in Britain's high case numbers.

Social Care Tragedy

But the biggest tragedy has undoubtedly been the crisis in care homes. Nearly a third of all COVID deaths have been among residents. From the start of the pandemic- when hospitals emptied their wards of countless untested patients into nursing homes – social care has been badly handled. Agency workers travelled from home to home, accelerating the spread of the virus, testing was rolled out too slowly and when the vaccine finally arrived its deployment was also too slow.

Unprepared NHS

Last February, when coronavirus was killing thousands in China, Health Secretary Matt Hancock said: 'Our world-class NHS is well prepared and we are doing everything we can to protect the public'. He was clearly wrong – the NHS was anything but prepared. By early April intensive care wards were overrun, protective equipment was in short supply and deaths were running at more than 1,000 a day. For years doctors have warned the

NHS is badly resourced. England, for example, has just ten intensive care beds per 100,000 people – Germany has 34. The issues are structural and fundamental reform is needed.

Ageing Population

Our ageing population has meant a far greater number of people were vulnerable to COVID than in younger nations. Age is, by far, the biggest risk factor for COVID deaths. Someone aged 85 to 89, for example, has an 8.9 per cent chance of dying if infected. For someone aged between 70 and 74, the risk is 2.3 per cent. This explains why wealthy countries have generally fared worse than developing ones where populations tend to be young.

Population Density

Britain has 273 people for every square kilometre – more than twice the European average of 108. One study, by the George Mason University in Fairfax, Virginia, predicted that population density accounts for 84 per cent of the difference between infection rates in different areas.

Fat Man of Europe

Obesity, diabetes and heart disease all increase the risk of faring badly if infected with Coronavirus. Britain has one of the worst obesity problems in Europe, with one in every three children and two in three adults overweight. Some 7.6 million people suffer from heart disease. Five million have diabetes.

It's Not All Bad News

Britain's scientists have led the charge over the last year and provided the world with hope for the future. The NHS carried out the Pioneer trial which in June discovered the first treatment to work against the virus, saving tens of thousands of lives around the world. And a team at Oxford developed one of the first COVID vaccines in record time. While the EU bickers with drugs firms, Britain is getting on

with its vaccination programme, with more than one in ten adults already immunised. So while the UK has much to regret about the last year, it can look to the future with hope".
Author: Ben Spencer, Analysis, Daily Mail, 27 January 2021, Page 7.

Commentary – We'll Never Have Zero COVID. But Yes, I Believe The End Is In Sight

"Has the beast been tamed? Could the end of COVID really be in sight? The numbers certainly look promising. Yesterday, it emerged that new daily infections had fallen in England for six days in a row. The numbers had plummeted 38 per cent week on week, with deaths happily down 24 per cent. Every English region saw a significant drop in new infections. The ever-gloomy modellers at the government's scientific advisory committee, Sage, had warned that new cases could reach 100,000 per day by the start of August, with 'Professor Lock-Down' Neil Ferguson even suggesting this could surge to 200,000 per day. Yet, yesterday, fewer than 25,000 positive tests were reported: less than a quarter of Sage's prediction. Even more reassuringly, unlike the first two waves, the new cases are not translating into a surge in hospitalisations or deaths – just 14 deaths were reported yesterday, down almost a quarter on the week before.

Last week, when the Prime Minister decided to lift the remaining official COVID restrictions, he was accused by critics of indulging in a 'reckless' experiment that could result in the virus spreading like wildfire across Britain, threatening the NHS. But the deadly conflagration has yet to spark. So far, 'Freedom Day' does not appear to have liberated the virus to kill people unchecked – and nor, crucially, does it look that any kind of lock-down will have to be reimposed in September, as some have warned. In fact, assuming the vaccines continue to work – and allowing for future 'booster' shots and tweaking the jabs to deal with new variants, there should be no reason ever to undergo a

COVID lock-down again. All this is exactly the outcome I forecast in early June, when there was a fierce public debate about the potential dangers of relaxing controls.

As a specialist in risk management, I have created a statistical model which I believe could both track the behaviour of the virus and predict what lay ahead. This model is much simpler than the methods adopted by some of the key Sage members, most notably Ferguson, and his team at Imperial College, London. It is based on just three factors: the size of the population, the average time taken by an infected person to pass on the virus, and the number of people infected by every person with COVID. Based on my findings, I argued that Britain would see large case numbers this summer, but far fewer hospitalisations and deaths than during the first two waves. In an article in the *Spectator* magazine, I wrote: 'The NHS should not come close to being overwhelmed. Cases will be mainly among the young, who are less likely to get seriously sick – so daily deaths will run at a quarter of what they once did before subsiding'.

I added that there was no point in delaying the great unlocking, because COVID-19 had been downgraded to a nasty bug, no more lethal than the flu. And that is the course that has been followed. If anything, in some areas my model has turned out to be slightly more pessimistic than the welcome reality. Let me be clear. The decline in new cases is real. Some have asserted that falls in new cases over the past week or so are due to factors including fewer tests being carried out, schools being closed over the summer or people going on holiday. My model has corrected for all of those factors – and it still shows cases falling. COVID is not yet over, of course. This third wave will continue to see large numbers of people being infected with the virus. On July 22, about 1.05 million people in England were estimated to have active COVID infections, close to the previous peak in December 2020, when the total reached 1.1 million. That number may rise significantly higher in the coming weeks, perhaps even approaching two million. Although that sounds like an alarming number, unlike the past two waves, there is no reason to panic.

Thanks in part to the phenomenal vaccine programme, the third and current wave of the virus is far less lethal than the previous two, just as my model predicted. After all, large numbers of these cases are asymptomatic: many people, particularly young and healthy ones, are not aware they even have COVID. As for hospitalisations, on July 20, 805 people in England were admitted to hospital with the virus. My model predicts a peak of about 1,000. This is a quarter of the 4,000 daily admissions we saw at the peak of the second wave. It is the same story with deaths. I forecast an average of 88 deaths per day for the week that has just passed. In the event, I was slightly pessimistic: the recorded average was actually 62. By mid-August, this rate could rise to some 250 deaths per day, but that would still be barely a fifth of the daily deaths that Britain saw in mid-January at the peak of the second wave – and when about 1,500 people die in Britain every day of all causes.

In the spring, Chief Medical Officer Chris Whitty suggested that 'any new surges will meet a wall of vaccinated people'. He was right. The vaccines have transformed COVID, providing a high degree of protection to the public, particularly to older people who are the most vulnerable to the disease. In every age band over 55, the take-up rates have been above 94 per cent, reaching 100 per cent in some cohorts, such as those aged 75 to 79. Among those most at risk, there has been no 'vaccine hesitancy' at all – and the consequences have been obvious. In January, all age groups were getting infected equally. Now just one in ten cases occurs among the over-65s. Younger people are currently less likely to have been vaccinated and are thus more likely to contract the disease.

For most of them, fortunately, it will just resemble a bad cold or a bout of flu. This has always been the case. Combined with the large numbers of people who have had COVID and recovered or perhaps were not even aware that they had been infected in the first place, the vaccines mean the population of Britain now has remarkably high levels of full immunity, perhaps up to some 94 per cent of adults in England. So, given all this, I do believe it is not too optimistic to hope that the virus has almost run its course in England. We will never entirely eradicate it – 'Zero COVID' will remain a fantasy. But, at least in this country, the worst of the pandemic is long over, and the end is very much in sight."

Author: Philip Thomas, is a visiting academic professor at Bristol University. Daily Mail, 27 July 2021, page 18.

References

Publications

Anderson, RM & May, RM, "Vaccination and Herd Immunity to Infectious Diseases" *Nature*, 1985, 318, 323-9.

Bailey, NJ, *The Mathematical Theory of Epidemics* (Charles Griffin & Co, London, 1957).

Collier L and Oxford, JS, *Human Virology: A Text for Students of Medicine* (Oxford University Press, 2006).

Holding, D, *A Warning from History: The Influenza Pandemic of 1918* (Scott Martin Productions, 2020).

Palmer, B, *Risky Numbers: The National Reporting of COVID-19* (Nuffield Trust, 2020).

Scobie, S, *Measuring Mortality during COVID-19: A Question and Answer*, (Nuffield Trust, 2021).

Research Papers

COVID-19 and Society (The British Academy, 2021).

Quarterly Review of Biophysics Discovery, June 2020.

Coronavirus and the Impact on Students in Higher Education (Office for National Statistics, December, 2020).

'COVID-19: Isolation having detrimental impact on children's education and welfare, particularly the most vulnerable' (Office for Standards in Education, *Third Report*, 2020).

Media Sources

BBC online news
Daily Mail
The Times
The Financial Times
The Economist
British Medical Journal
The Lancet

Online Sources

www.bbc.co.uk/news/coronavirus
www.gov.uk/government/collections/ – covid covid-19, vaccinations
www.gov.uk (2020) – The 'R' number in the UK
www.ons.gov.uk/ – COVID-19 Infection Survey
www.worldometers.info/coronavirus/country/uk/
www.statistica.com/uk-coronavirus data
www.ukdataservice.ac.uk
www.nhs.uk/statistics/covid-19-and-the-production-of-statistics/
phengland.co.uk/covid-19 statistics
www.bmj.com/coronavirus

* 9 7 9 8 4 5 0 3 4 2 8 4 9 *